T0318475

Cambridge Elements ≡

Elements in Public and Nonprofit Administration
edited by
Andrew Whitford
University of Georgia
Robert Christensen
Brigham Young University

WHEN GOVERNMENTS LOBBY GOVERNMENTS

The Institutional Origins of Intergovernmental Persuasion in America

Youlang Zhang
Renmin University of China

Shaftesbury Road, Cambridge CB2 8EA, United Kingdom

One Liberty Plaza, 20th Floor, New York, NY 10006, USA

477 Williamstown Road, Port Melbourne, VIC 3207, Australia

314–321, 3rd Floor, Plot 3, Splendor Forum, Jasola District Centre,
New Delhi – 110025, India

103 Penang Road, #05–06/07, Visioncrest Commercial, Singapore 238467

Cambridge University Press is part of Cambridge University Press & Assessment,
a department of the University of Cambridge.

We share the University's mission to contribute to society through the pursuit of
education, learning and research at the highest international levels of excellence.

www.cambridge.org
Information on this title: www.cambridge.org/9781009108386

DOI: 10.1017/9781009104180

First published 2022

A catalogue record for this publication is available from the British Library.

ISBN 978-1-009-10838-6 Paperback
ISSN 2515-4303 (online)
ISSN 2515-429X (print)

When Governments Lobby Governments

The Institutional Origins of Intergovernmental Persuasion in America

Elements in Public and Nonprofit Administration

DOI: 10.1017/9781009104180
First published online: December 2022

Youlang Zhang
Renmin University of China
Author for correspondence: Youlang Zhang, zhangyoulang@ruc.edu.cn

Abstract: Why are some subnational governments more likely to lobby the national government than others? Extant research in social sciences has widely discussed lobbying dynamics in the private sector. However, governments lobby governments too. In the United States, lobbying is a popular strategy for state and local governments to obtain resources from and influence policies in the federal government. Nevertheless, extant research offers limited theoretical analysis or empirical evidence on this phenomenon. This Element provides a comprehensive study of intergovernmental lobbying activities in the United States and, in particular, an institutional analysis of the lobbying decisions of state and local governments. The study findings contribute to public administration, public policy, and political science literature by offering theoretical and empirical insights into the institutional factors that might influence subnational policymaking, fiscal resource management, intergovernmental relations, and democratic representation.

Keywords: lobbying, institution, intergovernmental relations, public finance, bureaucratic politics

ISBNs: 9781009108386 (PB), 9781009104180 (OC)
ISSNs: 2515-4303 (online), 2515-429X (print)

Contents

1 Introduction

1.1 Intergovernmental Lobbying in the United States

An important question in public administration, public policy, and political science is how different individuals and groups can influence government policymaking through lobbying (Grose et al. 2022; Hall and Deardorff 2006; Kingdon 1984; Yackee 2020; You 2017). Lobbying is one of the most common approaches to gaining political influence. It refers to "the transfer of information in private meetings and venues between interest groups and politicians, their staffs, and agents" (De Figueiredo and Richter 2014, p. 164). The right of individuals, groups, and corporations to lobby the federal government was supported by the founding fathers of the United States, such as James Madison in the *Federalist Papers* in 1788, and later formally protected by the right to petition in the First Amendment to the United States Constitution in 1791. To influence public officials, interest groups can either hire professional lobbyists or lobby them directly (Gray and Lowery 1996; Walker 1983, 1991). Like private groups, state and local governments have spent tens of millions of dollars annually hiring professional lobbyists to make lobbying contacts with federal officials in Washington DC, in recent years (Goldstein and You 2017; Payson 2020a, 2020b). In general, intergovernmental lobbying has become an essential strategy for state and local governments to obtain resources from and influence policies in the federal government (Martin 1990; Nixon 1944; Pelissero and England 1987).

However, the lobbying activities of subnational governments remain poorly understood. The following questions have not been adequately explored and answered. What determines a subnational government's participation in lobbying the federal government? Why do some subnational governments invest more resources in lobbying the federal government than others? Given a multilevel federalist government structure in the United States, how do the lobbying decisions of local governments affect those of state governments? This study primarily aims to shed new light on these questions by identifying and testing the institutional origins of intergovernmental lobbying decisions. In this Element, intergovernmental lobbying refers to the lobbying contacts between different levels of governments, which do not include interbranch lobbying within a government unless otherwise stated.

Understanding the logic of intergovernmental lobbying is crucial because it has important theoretical, normative, and practical implications. Theoretically, exploring the institutional origins of intergovernmental lobbying can aid in comprehending government policymaking, fiscal decisions, and intergovernmental relations (Jensen 2018), important theoretical topics in public administration, public finance, public policy, and political science. Normatively, intergovernmental lobbying may significantly affect socioeconomic equity. In the literature on private lobbying, an important concern of the private interest groups is that citizens with more money and better political connections may exert more influence than others (Hayes 1981; Schattschneider and Adamany 1975). Similarly, subnational governments are incentivized to influence the process of intergovernmental resource allocation through lobbying. Therefore, the current democratic representation system might also favor certain subnational governments and create political, economic, and social inequity across jurisdictions. Finally, practically, previous literature reveals that some subnational governments have an undue lobbying advantage over other governments (Goldstein and You 2017; Payson 2020a, 2020b). A theoretical and empirical analysis of the determinants of intergovernmental lobbying can help reformers regulate lobbying activities more effectively and limit the unequal distribution of access to federal officials among subnational governments.

Prior research has employed two general approaches to the study of lobbying. The first approach focuses on the strategies or consequences of lobbying. For instance, formal theorists have modeled lobbying as vote-buying, informative signaling, or legislative subsidy (Ellis and Groll 2020; Hall and Deardorff 2006; Schnakenberg and Turner 2019). Empiricists have tested the effects of lobbying on policy decisions, earmark appropriations, or shareholder value (Borisov, Goldman, and Gupta 2016; De Figueiredo and Silverman 2006; Haeder and Yackee 2015; Kollman 1997; Yackee 2006; Yackee and Yackee 2006; You 2017). Normative researchers argue that interest group politics could undermine political equity and the interests of broad publics (Hayes 1981, 1992; Schlozman 1984).

The second approach to studying lobbying, which is more relevant to this Element, focuses on the origins of lobbying activities. For instance, given the potential collective action problem inherent in lobbying, Olson (1965) points out that lobbying activities are the by-products of groups designed for other economic or social functions. Specifically, these groups should "(1) have the authority and capacity to be coercive, or (2) have a source of positive inducements that they can offer the individuals in a latent group" (Olson 1965, p. 133). Similarly, based on Hirschman's (1970) Exit, Voice, and Loyalty (EVL) framework, Clark, Golder, and Golder (2017) developed a formal model and provided another explanation for citizens' choices of lobbying. Their EVL model with complete information suggests that sufficiently powerful citizens (with a credible exit threat) need not lobby because the government has already allocated adequate resources to them. Citizens who lack power (without a credible exit threat) choose not to lobby because they know the government will ignore them. Clark, Golder, and Golder (2017) also suggested a pooling equilibrium in which both powerful and powerless citizens choose to lobby when there is incomplete information on the part of a government.

Although mainly based on private groups' lobbying activities and simplistic assumptions (Dekel, Jackson, and Wolinsky 2009; Olson 1965; Stigler 1971), these explanations provide important insights into the incentives and constraints behind lobbying activities. Nevertheless, we still need to account for specific institutional incentives, capacity, and opportunities in the public sector to develop an intuitive and contextual explanation for intergovernmental lobbying.

Although limited scholarly attention is paid to public lobbying than private lobbying, qualitative research on intergovernmental lobbying has persisted for decades. For instance, American politics and public administration scholars have provided broad descriptions of the lobbying functions of the *big seven* (the US conference of mayors, the international city/county management association, the national leagues of cities, the national association of counties, the national governors' conference, the council of state governments, and the national conference of state legislatures) or subnational governments' lobbying offices in Washington DC (Brooks 1961; Cammisa 1995; Farkas 1971; Haider 1974; Hays 1991; Herian 2011; Jensen 2016; Jensen and Emery 2011; Leckrone 2019; Palazzolo and McCarthy 2005). These qualitative studies may help us understand the history or operations of government lobbying activities. However, they cannot help us systematically identify the determinants of government lobbying decisions through a rigorous research design.

Nevertheless, due to the increasing availability of professional lobbying data, several quantitative studies on intergovernmental lobbying have appeared in recent years. After the US Congress approved the Lobbying Disclosure Act (LDA) in 1995, all professional lobbying contacts with an expense higher than $10,000 were required to be registered. The Clerk of the US House of Representatives and the Secretary of the US Senate are responsible for the registration, filing, and compilation of reports submitted by the lobbyists (Straus 2017). A few watchdog organizations (e.g., Center for Responsive Politics or CRP) or scholars (e.g., Kim 2017) have attempted to collect, digitize, and classify millions of these lobbying reports to create publicly available lobbying databases (e.g., CRP's OpenSecrets.org and Kim's LobbyView.org). Based on CRP's database, Loftis and Kettler (2015) analyzed the lobbying activities of 498 cities between 1998 and 2008 and found that economic distress (measured by cities' unemployment rate) pushed cities to lobby the federal government. Further, the competitiveness of congressional districts was positively associated with spending on lobbying. Goldstein and You (2017) built a dataset of cities with populations over 25,000 between 1999 and 2012. They argued that the underprovision of public goods increased cities' participation and investment in lobbying the federal government. Payson (2020b) analyzed a dataset of 1,200 cities in 50 states from 2006 to 2014 and found that the partisan mismatch between a city and its state representative played a significant role in motivating lobbying efforts.

Almost all previous explanations for intergovernmental lobbying have considered a local government a unitary actor seeking only to satisfy local public demands or assume that intergovernmental lobbying decisions could be completely inferred by observing jurisdictional characteristics such as socioeconomic demands or partisanship. For instance, Loftis and Kettler (2015), Goldstein and You (2017), and Payson (2020b) argue that local governments increase their lobbying investments because they need extra resources from the federal government to meet the demands of local citizens. However, presumably, every rational local government would prefer more resources from the federal government regardless of the actual level of public demand. Why do not all cities choose to lobby the federal government? Why do some local governments invest more resources in lobbying the federal government than others? Owing to limited resources and the political priorities of decision-makers, governments do not necessarily invest in all activities that might produce positive returns (Bertelli and John 2013; Nicholson-Crotty 2015). Even if lobbying is lucrative (Goldstein and You 2017; Payson 2020a), a theory to explain local lobbying decisions apart from public demands should also consider the institutions that potentially determine the incentives and constraints of policymakers in subnational governments. This study aims to develop and test such institutional explanations.

Two types of lobbying activities – formal and informal – should be distinguished before any further analysis is conducted (Jensen 2018). Formal lobbying refers to how clients hire professional lobbyists to make lobbying contacts with government officials. Specifically, the LDA defines a professional lobbyist as an individual who makes at least one lobbying contact quarterly, is compensated, and spends at least 20 percent of their time on lobbying activities. Informal lobbying refers to how clients directly communicate with government officials through informal contacts, such as private letters, phone calls, or meetings. "Incidental lobbying" or "shadow lobbying" (as commonly defined by national and state lobbying laws) may also be viewed as a form of informal lobbying. This is because it refers to the activities of a person engaged in lobbying activities for only a few hours or someone who makes only a few lobbying expenditures and, therefore, is not required to register as a lobbyist (Akiashvili et al. 2018; LaPira 2015).

Consistent with previous empirical research (Goldstein and You 2017; Loftis and Kettler 2015; Payson 2020a, 2020b), this study explicitly limits the analysis of intergovernmental lobbying to formal lobbying to improve logical consistency and avoid unnecessary theoretical or empirical confusion. The study provides two justifications for this choice. First, it is difficult (or impossible) to systematically collect and analyze evidence of informal lobbying, as participants are not likely to publicly report the details of their activities. Conversely, studying formal lobbying activities is a more practical way of conducting systematic analysis and statistical inference and gaining convincing empirical insights. Second, in general, informal lobbying is likely to be correlated with formal lobbying despite its lower visibility in politics. Federal officials tend to have limited knowledge of each specific policy issue and limited attention, time, or resources allocation to various policy issues (Alesina and Tabellini 2007, 2008; Wilensky 2015). Direct informal contact with a federal official may serve the function of political signaling. However, these informal contacts are not likely to have a substantive effect without hiring professional lobbyists familiar with federal policy issues and schedules and have abundant political contacts to provide the corresponding legislative subsidies (Hall and Deardoff 2006). In other words, professional lobbying information, although limited, might be a reasonable proxy of all formal and informal lobbying activities.

1.2 Qualitative Observations

Understanding how lobbying works in practice is important in developing theoretical arguments and implementing the design of this empirical research. To substantiate my knowledge of professional lobbying activities in practice, I went to Washington DC, to observe how local officials lobby federal officials with the help of professional lobbyists. I conducted a series of personal interviews with them in the spring of 2018. Further, I collected and analyzed dozens of electronic or hardcopy lobbying manuals edited by private lobbyists whom I interviewed, the association of government relations professionals, and members of the American Bar Association (Gordon and Susman 2009). Although these qualitative observations do not directly constitute empirical research, they provide necessary contextual information for this study's main research topic and research designs. More importantly, they could facilitate the development of logically consistent and empirically convincing arguments throughout this Element.

A common myth about the professional lobbying industry might be that lobbyists spend most of their time having fancy dinners with politicians and trying to shape politicians' policy positions through direct persuasion or interest exchange. However, in real life, most professional lobbyists have to spend most of their time researching legislative or administrative matters, attending strategy sessions, making telephone calls, and preparing policy proposals and plans for lobbying communications. Lobbyists also need to understand the congressional policy schedule (e.g., the expiration or renewal date of bills), the schedules of federal officials and their staff, funding availability for programs, and federal officials' policy positions. In fact, according to my interviews, private lobbyists working for local governments tend to identify themselves as "babysitters" or "city employees."

As Baumgartner et al. (2009, p. 22) suggested, "Attention in Washington is scarce." Politicians are extremely busy with various types of political matters (e.g., floor votes, committee votes, or hundreds of meeting requests a day) and often only have limited knowledge on specific policy issues. Therefore, politicians often hire dozens or even hundreds of legislative staff with different types of expertise to deal with visitors from various backgrounds and work on those professional issues. The most common form of lobbying occurs through delivering policy information or proposals to staff working in politicians' offices. For instance, during my trip to Capitol Hill, I observed that local officials from Texas only had thirty seconds to take a photo with Senator John Cornyn during the senators' weekly meeting with his supporters, called Texas Thursday Coffee. Conversely, during the typical formal lobbying process, local officials, with the guidance of professional lobbyists, have approximately fifteen minutes to communicate policy messages with a staff assistant, legislative correspondent, or legislative director from the office of a representative or a senator. The policy messages may include the policy background, actions requested, suggested legislative language, and issue importance in each federal official's electoral district.

The legislative staff who work for federal officials tend to have professional knowledge regarding specific policy issues, and they draft the policy documents for federal officials. Therefore, direct lobbying to legislative staff is not necessarily less effective than direct communication with a federal official. Of course, lobbyists need to adjust their language and strategies according to each congressional district and the policy position of each federal official. However, an informal rule in the formal lobbying process is that conversations between local officials, lobbyists, and legislative staff should stay on the main policy messages. They should not include campaign donations or other topics that may imply direct interest exchange or provoke legal risks.

The qualitative data, including field observations, interviews, and secondary materials, show that intergovernmental formal lobbying services involve several typical characteristics.

First, formal lobbying activities tend to involve high transaction costs for the clients, including broad information, bargaining, and enforcement costs. Information costs include understanding the requirements of local communities, finding an appropriate lobbying firm with relevant expertise and connections, and determining the firm's conditions. The bargaining costs include negotiating a price with the lobbying firm. The enforcement costs include coordinating with lobbyists to improve the effectiveness of lobbying activities, such as designing lobbying strategies or policy proposals. Moreover, typical principal-agent problems such as information asymmetry and interest conflicts are commonplace in the lobbying market. Simply paying a lobbyist a lump sum and asking them to lobby may lead to moral hazards, such as in the *2006 Jack Abramoff Native American Lobbying Scandal*, when lobbyists successfully overbilled and then secretly lobbied against their clients due to a lack of supervision (Abramoff 2011). Therefore, clients also need to monitor the behavior of lobbyists to ensure lobbying services are delivered as promised.

Second, clients' inputs or the prices of hiring professional lobbyists are immediate and definite. Professional lobbyists are employed because of their knowledge of the intricacies of the policy process, including "who to talk to, how and when to present an effective argument, and what needs to be done to follow-up."[1] Generally, professional lobbyists need to provide three types of information to federal officials: political details on the status or prospect of government decisions, career-related information about government officials' own jobs, and analytical policy information about the social consequences of government decisions (Nownes 2006). Therefore, many lobbyists choose to work as staff in Congress to establish extensive political connections before they work for the lobbying firms. Further, lobbyists tend to have an academic degree in political science, public administration, public policy, law, or economics. They spend years studying one or several specific policy issues such as agriculture, transportation, education, environment, or defense to become well-known policy experts on these issues in Washington DC (Bertrand, Bombardini, and Trebbi 2014; McCrain 2018; Shepherd and You 2020). Therefore, clients have to pay more to hire a lobbyist with more connections or a higher level of expertise (Bertrand, Bombardini, and Trebbi 2014; McCrain 2018; Vidal, Draca, and Fons-Rosen 2012). To formally lobby the federal government, local governments have to directly allocate fiscal resources from their budgets for signing contracts with professional lobbyists.

---

[1] AGRP, "Voice of the Lobbying, Public Policy, and Advocacy Professions." http://grprofessionals .org/about-association-government-relations-professionals

Third, the outputs of formal lobbying tend to be produced in the long term and are uncertain (Baumgartner et al. 2009; Nownes 2006). Lobbying is a long-term game that requires repeated interactions to build mutual trust between clients, lobbyists, and officials. Most formal lobbying activities occur through providing a government official with legislative or policy support rather than applying direct persuasion or interest exchange (Baumgartner et al. 2009; Hall and Deardoff 2006). Thus, a consequence of city lobbying is to increase the salience of a city on the federal policy agenda, although it usually does not produce a quick payoff. My observations in DC and evidence from the existing literature (Kingdon 1984; Nownes 2006; Straus 2015) show that the most direct purpose of lobbying is to keep federal officials informed of local government policy issues (i.e., brand building) and track their sentiment for specific issues. Recent research suggests that endorsements from well-connected interest groups provide a strong cue for federal officials with limited information early in the policymaking process (Box-Steffensmeier, Christenson, and Craig 2019). Such interest groups wield less direct influence when bills progress.

Moreover, there are several sources of uncertainties in lobbying returns. Lobbyists often produce little change if they meet equal opposition to their efforts or find that space on the federal policy agenda is scarce (Baumgartner et al. 2009). This situation does not mean that lobbyists' efforts are useless as their clients may also benefit from the policy status quo. Baumgartner et al. (2009) even suggest that the most common goal of lobbying is to protect an existing policy from a proposed change. Additionally, despite local public demands, the choice of lobbying issues depends largely on congressional schedules or the emergence of focusing events or "policy windows" such as the expiration date of bills (e.g., the farm bill renews every five years) and funding availability. Finally, even if the federal government responds to the lobbying efforts of a local government with more fiscal or policy support, the supply of this federal support may not precisely match the demands of the local government, which further increases the uncertainty of lobbying output.

1.3 Overview of Sections

This Element comprises five sections. Section 1 briefly introduces intergovernmental lobbying in the United States and reviews the existing literature on this topic. Moreover, understanding how lobbying works in practice provides a basis for developing theoretical arguments and implementing empirical research design. Therefore, this section also includes qualitative observations.

Section 2 proposes that cities with professional executives (i.e., council-manager cities) are more likely than those with political executives (i.e., mayor-council cities) to hire professional lobbyists. In terms of motivation, professional executives have longer time horizons or lower discount rates than political executives due to their job stability and lifelong careers; thus, higher returns on lobbying investment are expected. In terms of capability, compared to political executives, whose attention is concentrated on reelections, professional executives are more capable of overcoming the transaction costs involved in lobbying given their previous professional training and rich experience in public service. This study provides an analysis of more than 1,200 cities between 1999 and 2012 in order to test this key hypothesis.

Section 3 presents the argument that legislative professionalism is positively associated with state governments' participation or investment in formally lobbying of the federal government. More professional state legislatures have more political channels to collect information from voters and are more likely to represent the preferences of the median voters (Carsey, Winburn, and Berry 2017). Therefore, state policymakers in a highly professional state legislature are more likely to allocate resources to lobbying for additional federal resources to meet the demands of median voters. Further, state governments with a high level of legislative professionalism will have more resources to overcome the transaction costs involved in employing professional lobbyists and thus have more access to lobbying services. I test this hypothesis using evidence from a panel dataset covering all fifty states from 1999 to 2011.

Building on Shipan and Volden's (2006) analysis of local-to-state policy diffusion, Section 4 points out that bottom-up federalism also exists in intergovernmental formal lobbying. Additionally, the intensity of local governments lobbying the federal government may have two distinct types of impact on the intensity of state governments lobbying the federal government: the snowball effect and the pressure valve effect. Regarding the snowball effect, local lobbying spending may increase state lobbying spending by increasing the salience of lobbying as a policy tool, producing negative externalities among local governments, or escalating the competition for scarce federal funding between state and local governments. Concerning the pressure valve effect, local lobbying spending may decrease state lobbying spending by obtaining additional resources to meet the demands of local voters and groups successfully and, therefore, decrease the policy pressures on state-level policymakers. Using a dataset of all fifty states from 1999 to 2011, this study provides evidence that local lobbying spending increases state lobbying spending (through a snowball effect) after controlling for political, financial, and demographic characteristics.

Finally, Section 5 concludes this Element by highlighting the main findings, discussing theoretical and practical implications, and pointing out potential directions for future research.

2 Executive Institutions and Lobbying Activities of City Governments

2.1 Theoretical Analysis

In recent years, at least 300 city governments spent millions of dollars annually formally lobbying the federal government and submitted at least one lobbying report under the LDA. Like interest groups in the private sector, city governments have their own special interests in terms of funding, policies, or autonomy (Farkas 1971). This section provides an explanation that illustrates the institutional incentives and constraints of city government executives when making lobbying decisions to improve our understanding of the determinants of intergovernmental lobbying.

Figure 1 shows how executive institutions affect local government decisions regarding formal lobbying. Most government executives in American cities are

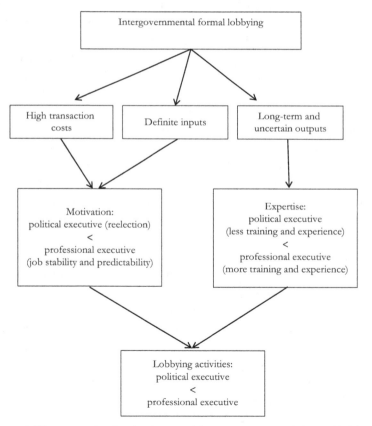

Figure 1 City executive institutions and intergovernmental formal lobbying decisions.

created in two ways (Hayes and Chang 1990; Krause et al. 2019). In mayor-council cities, the government executives are the elected mayors; in council-manager cities, the government executives are hired professional city managers. Both political (i.e., elected mayors) and professional (i.e., hired city managers) executives oversee the general operations of city governments and are widely involved in the budgeting and management of local governments (Svara 1999). In particular, managing intergovernmental relations is a significant responsibility of local government executives.[2] Numerous urban politics studies suggest that executive institutions significantly affect various types of local policy decisions (Carr 2015; Clingermayer and Feiock 2001; Feiock, Jeong, and Kim 2003; Krause et al. 2019; Lubell, Feiock, and De La Cruz 2009). Therefore, it is reasonable to expect that both types of government executives significantly affect cities' decisions regarding hiring professionals to lobby the federal government.

Following an institutional rational choice perspective (Weingast 1996; Weingast, Shepsle, and Johnsen 1981), this study has the following two assumptions: (1) government executives are rational in the sense of maximizing their career benefits; and (2) institutions create incentives and constraints to shape executives' rational choices. Given the three typical attributes of professional lobbying services (high transaction costs, definite inputs, and long-term and uncertain outputs) discussed in Section 1, this study argues that political and professional executives have different motivations and expertise and make different cost-benefit decisions in terms of lobbying the federal government.

Professional executives tend to have a stronger motivation than political executives to invest in formal intergovernmental lobbying activities. Political executives generally have a shorter time horizon and a higher discount rate in terms of lobbying investments. First, political executives are directly accountable to voters before the next election and are likely to focus opportunistically on short-term voter demands rather than the long-term outputs produced by lobbying (Feiock, Jeong, and Kim 2003). Second, political executives and council members are directly elected by voters and, therefore, are not accountable to each other. They can choose to blame each other for noncooperation if a city government does not perform well (Mullin, Peele, and Cain 2004). The costs of lobbying are immediate, definite, and easily visible, while the benefits of lobbying are less visible and mostly in the long term. Therefore, it is difficult for political executives to take credit and easy for them to be attacked by

---

[2] For instance, in the city of Los Angeles, the mayor works with the community liaison office to maintain effective relationships with other governments. http://cao.lacity.org/budget/. Managing intergovernmental relations is repeatedly listed as a key issue in the annual strategic plans of the city manager's office of College Station, Texas. www.cstx.gov/index.aspx?page=16

political opponents for investing money, resources, or time in formal lobbying. Thus, political executives might opportunistically prefer highly visible short-term projects (e.g., public schools) to less visible long-term projects (e.g., lobbying the federal government) to maintain their political careers (Bueno 2021; Krause et al. 2019; Olson 1993).

Conversely, professional executives tend to have longer and more stable careers (Zhang 2007) and, therefore, have a lower discount rate regarding lobbying benefits. Although there is no systematic data on the tenure of all city managers and mayors in the United States in the past decades, the existing research provides some small-sample evidence to suggest that city managers have longer tenures than mayors. For instance, based on a dataset of 120 cities, Ammons and Bosse (2005) found that the average tenure of city managers was around seven years and had increased since the 1980s. Conversely, McNitt (2010) found that mayoral tenure was only approximately six years in nineteen major cities. Additionally, city managers often negotiate with city councils for severance protection (financial protection from termination without cause) or protection from termination before or after a local election. This situation increases councils' cost to terminate city managers and avoids career risk for the city managers (Connolly 2016).

Moreover, without being directly accountable to voters before the next election, professional managers' decisions are relatively insulated from the voters and can be made consistently (Feiock, Jeong, and Kim 2003; Ting 2021). Existing research shows that professional managers are relatively insensitive to the demands of the elected politicians and more often lead their elected politicians to the "right" policy in the broader professional community (Teodoro 2011). Furthermore, different from the political executives, who only serve as one (rather than multiple) city's government executives in their career as a politician, professional executives have a bigger potential job market; it is easier for them to move and serve another city. Therefore, to maintain or improve their career in the long term, professional executives have to serve two clients (Connolly 2016; Lei and Zhou 2022; Teodoro 2011): the current client who pays their salary and the potential client who may pay their salary in the future. Therefore, this stronger job predictability and broader job mobility determine that city managers have a longer time horizon for making lobbying decisions and initiating intergovernmental contacts.

From the perspective of expertise, professional executives have a lower transaction cost than political executives when lobbying the federal government. The decisions of government executives are significantly influenced by their knowledge, skills, and experience (Kirkland 2021; Lynn 1987). To improve the effectiveness of formal lobbying, government executives need to take advantage of their policy knowledge and managerial experience to facilitate the process of choosing issues, making plans, signing contracts, and coordinating with professional lobbyists, and so on. Political executives are usually relatively inexperienced in terms of policy or administration when they assume office, as their previous professional backgrounds tend to be varied and unrelated to public service (Kirkland 2021). Further, local electoral campaigns occupy a significant share of political executives' attention, time, staff, and resources. Therefore, political executives probably have less professional experience or knowledge necessary for facilitating professional lobbying.

Conversely, professional executives are generally professionally trained (e.g., they may have a bachelor's or master's degree in public administration or public policy) and have multiple years of municipal management experience before being hired as city managers (Carr 2015; Carreri and Payson 2021). As full-time professionals, professional executives accumulate considerable knowledge, skill, and administration experience in local policy issues, funding methods, and bureaucratic communication and control skills, which are important for determining the need for lobbying in cities and the bureaucratic resources required for lobbying. Many existing studies have shown that city managers devote more time to policy and administration than elected mayors (Carr 2015). Therefore, even if a political and a professional executive have the same motivation and resources for lobbying the federal government, the professional executive could more effectively facilitate the lobbying process.

The above analysis leads to the same conclusion – all things being equal, compared to cities with political executives, cities with professional executives are more likely to invest resources in formally lobbying the federal government. Therefore, I suggest the following hypothesis.

Key Hypothesis: Cities with professional executives are more likely than those with political executives to invest resources in formally lobbying the federal government.

2.2 Evidence

Ideally, to test this section's key argument, each city's participation and overall investment in lobbying other governments should be used as the dependent variables. However, most cities' annual financial reports do not directly list the specific amount of money spent on lobbying, and there is no established lobbying budgeting database. Although cities' investments in lobbying the state governments are generally available on each state's website, the data are

hard to collect. Moreover, variations in disclosure requirements such as differ-
ential compensation, reimbursement, or expenditure thresholds make it difficult
to compare lobbying data across different states. This study examined the
impact of executive institutions on cities' lobbying decisions by focusing on
cities' lobbying activities at the federal level. The main reason is that the LDA
requires all interest groups who contribute more than $10,000 to lobbying the
federal government to file lobbying disclosure reports.

The main dataset was developed based on the study of Goldstein and You
(2017). The dataset covers cities with a population greater than 25,000 between
1999 and 2012. The unit of analysis is a city-year. The original sample com-
prised 1,262 unique "cities." However, a closer examination of the dataset
showed that three of the sampled units were census tracts or counties –
Montgomery in Maryland, Huntington Station in New York, and Boardman in
Ohio – rather than cities with a general-purpose government. These were
removed, and the final research sample included 1,259 cities.

There were two dependent variables of interest. I set the first dependent
variable as a dummy equal to 1 if a city submitted a federal lobbying report in
a year, and 0 if otherwise. I employed logit models to predict the binary
dependent variable. The second dependent variable of interest was the amount
a city government invested in lobbying the federal government. It was measured
with the natural log of the level of lobbying expense due to the highly skewed
distribution (see Figure 2; Borisov, Goldman, and Gupta 2016). Given the
nonnegative nature of the dependent variable and the LDA only requiring the
registration of any organization that contributes more than $10,000 toward
lobbying activities each year, I used a tobit model to analyze lobbying spending.
This dealt with the potential censoring problem among cities (Goldstein and
You 2017; Trounstine and Valdini 2008).

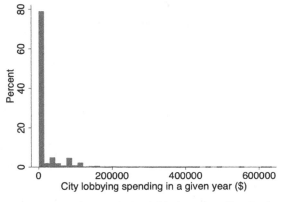

Figure 2 Histogram of annual city lobbying spending in the sample.

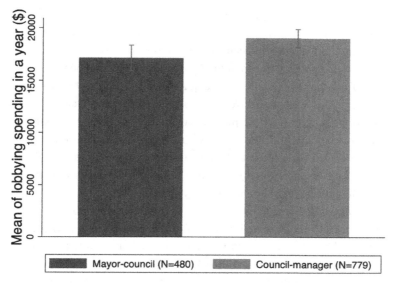

Figure 3 Average yearly lobbying spending of two types of cities.

For the second dependent variable, I did not use the percentage of lobbying expenses in each government's expenditure as a measure. This is because in a model with a ratio as the dependent variable, we do not know whether the independent variable has an impact on the numerator or the denominator. To isolate the effect of each government's expenditure, I chose to control for it on the right side of the equation.

The key independent variable is the executive institution of each city in the sample. I measured the executive institution with a dummy equal to 1 if a city has a council-manager form of government, and 0 otherwise. Figure 3 shows 779 council-manager cities and 480 mayor-council cities in the sample. On average, council-manager cities spend 2,000 more dollars on lobbying the federal government than mayor-council cities in a year. The institutional data came from surveys conducted by the International City/County Manager's Association (ICMA) in 1981, 1986, 1991, 1996, 2001, 2006, and 2011. Following De Benedictis-Kessner and Warshaw (2016), I used the most recent survey to which a city responded to measure its institutions. When there were missing data in ICMA surveys, I manually collected cities' most recent institutional information from their official government websites.

Other control variables were the demographic, financial, and political characteristics of sampled cities, as these variables may influence the motivations, obstacles, or resources for intergovernmental lobbying (Goldstein and You 2017). The demographic variables were population size, land area, water area, percentage of older adults (aged over sixty-five) in the population, percentage of students (aged five to seventeen) in the population, ethnic heterogeneity,[3] median household income, percentage of unemployed people, percentage of people below the poverty line, and the Gini index of income inequality. These data came from the Decennial Census and American Community Surveys. The financial variables were the differences between city- and state-level direct expenditure per capita (i.e., the public goods gap), the share of property tax, and intergovernmental transfer in a city's revenue. These data were collected from the Census of Governments. Finally, the political variables were the party affiliation of the house representatives and senators who represented the cities and the state governors (Shor and McCarty 2011).

Further, I included year fixed effects in the logit and tobit models to capture any time-specific trends. For instance, even-numbered years tend to have fewer new lobbyist registrations under the LDA than odd-numbered years due to the shifts in party control of the White House and Congress or those in the issue agenda resulting from elections (Straus 2015). The 2007 Honest Leadership and Open Government Act (LaPira and Thomas III 2014; Straus 2017) and the 2011 earmark ban may also have caused declines in lobbying activities (Kirk, Mallett, and Peterman 2017). Table 1 reports the summary statistics.

Table 2 shows the estimates of the determinants of lobbying participation across American cities. Given the logit model specifications, the odds ratios for one unit increase in each independent variable and t-statistics in parentheses are provided. The two-tailed p-values are shown in separate columns. Table 2 also reports the McFadden R^2 (McFadden 1974), the Akaike information criterion (AIC) (Akaike 1974), and the Bayesian information criterion (BIC) (Schwarz 1978). Further, Table 2 presents specifications with controls only alongside specifications that include executive institutions; the city-level executive institutions markedly improve model fit (Δ AIC –55 for Model 2), indicating that city lobbying participation varies significantly by city institutions.

The results are consistent with the key hypothesis. The results shown in Table 2 indicate that after controlling for the divergence between the city and state public goods provision, demographic characteristics, public finance conditions, and political variables, executive institutions are still significant predictors of a city participating in formal lobbying of the federal government. Council-manager cities are approximately 40 percent more likely than mayor-council cities to participate in formally lobbying the federal government.

---

[3] Ethnic heterogeneity is calculated using $1 - \sum_{i=1}^{n} p_i^2$ (i.e., the Gibbs–Martin index or Blau index), where p_i represents a share of an ethnicity i within a population.

Table 1 Summary statistics

Variable	Obs.	Mean	Std. Dev.	Min.	Max.
Lobbying participation	17,626	0.241	0.428	0.000	1.000
Lobbying spending logged	17,626	2.390	4.577	0.000	13.361
Council-manager	17,626	0.613	0.487	0.000	1.000
District-based elections	17,626	35.606	41.629	0.000	100.000
Initiative	17,626	0.655	0.475	0.000	1.000
Referendum	17,626	0.675	0.468	0.000	1.000
Recall	17,626	0.596	0.491	0.000	1.000
Public goods gap ($)	17,626	-2.165	1.237	-12.255	6.814
Population (1,000)	17,626	103.601	298.033	18.156	8,214.426
Land area (1,000 sq. miles)	17,626	0.040	0.108	0.001	2.717
Water area (1,000 sq. miles)	17,626	0.004	0.024	0.000	0.552
Senior (%)	17,626	12.396	4.247	2.553	37.776

Table 1 (cont.)

Variable	Obs.	Mean	Std. Dev.	Min.	Max.
Student (%)	17,626	17.573	3.558	2.523	31.856
Ethnic heterogeneity	17,626	0.385	0.167	0.037	0.784
Median income ($1,000)	17,626	58.259	21.855	22.303	192.777
Unemployment (%)	17,626	8.042	3.817	1.490	30.252
Households in poverty	17,626	10.828	6.901	0.526	38.146
Gini index	17,626	0.423	0.053	0.267	0.642
Property tax share of revenue	17,626	0.238	0.152	0.000	0.915
Intergovernmental transfer share of revenue	17,626	0.181	0.130	0.000	0.780
Democrat house representative	17,626	0.708	0.455	0.000	1.000
Democrat senator	17,626	0.603	0.418	0.000	1.000
Republican governor	17,626	0.518	0.500	0.000	1.000

Table 2 Determinants of lobbying participation across cities

	Model 1		Model 2	
	Odds ratio (*t*-statistic)	*p*-value	Odds ratio (*t*-statistic)	*p*-value
Council-manager			1.398 (2.50)	0.013
Public goods gap ($)	1.346 (4.19)	0.000	1.320 (3.89)	0.000
Population (1,000)	1.001 (0.60)	0.545	1.002 (0.65)	0.518
Land area (1,000 sq. miles)	18.03 (0.96)	0.336	18.43 (0.97)	0.333
Water area (1,000 sq. miles)	8.505 (0.64)	0.525	9.049 (0.68)	0.494
Senior (%)	0.957 (−2.66)	0.008	0.957 (−2.73)	0.006
Student (%)	1.051 (2.46)	0.014	1.047 (2.27)	0.023
Ethnic heterogeneity	4.776 (3.39)	0.001	4.080 (2.96)	0.003
Median income ($1,000)	0.991 (−1.83)	0.067	0.991 (−1.81)	0.071
Unemployment (%)	1.029 (1.47)	0.140	1.031 (1.60)	0.110
Households in poverty	0.964 (−2.45)	0.014	0.968 (−2.21)	0.027
Gini index	1,330.6 (5.14)	0.000	1,438.7 (5.23)	0.000
Property tax share of revenue	0.0792 (−5.57)	0.000	0.0879 (−5.23)	0.000
Intergovernmental transfer share of revenue	0.121 (−4.83)	0.000	0.164 (−3.98)	0.000
Democrat house representative	1.502 (2.90)	0.004	1.502 (2.90)	0.004

Table 2 (cont.)

	Model 1		Model 2	
	Odds ratio (*t*-statistic)	*p*-value	Odds ratio (*t*-statistic)	*p*-value
Democrat senator	1.862 (4.36)	0.000	1.837 (4.28)	0.000
Republican governor	1.136 (1.70)	0.090	1.144 (1.78)	0.075
Year fixed effects	Y		Y	
Constant	0.009 (−6.36)	0.000	0.006 (−6.62)	0.000
Observations	17,626		1,7626	
Pseudo R²	0.150		0.153	
AIC	16,596.4		16,541.5	
BIC	16,829.7		16,782.6	

Note: Two-tailed *p*-values. Logit models. The dependent variable is a dummy equal to 1 if a city submits a lobbying report in a year, and 0 otherwise. Models also include year dummies that are not reported. Cluster-robust standard errors are used (clustered at the city level).

Table 3 shows the models of federal lobbying spending by city governments. Given the tobit model specifications, the coefficients for one unit increase in each independent variable and robust standard errors clustered by cities in parentheses are provided. The two-tailed p-values are shown in separate columns. Table 3 also reports the McFadden R^2, AIC, and BIC. I ran two regressions. Model 3 includes all control variables, and Model 4 further includes the measure of executive institutions. City executive institutions markedly improve model fit (Δ AIC -39 for Model 4).

My test corroborates that executive institutions still significantly predict lobbying spending after controlling for the divergence between the city and state public goods provision, demographic characteristics, public finance conditions, and political variables. Specifically, compared to mayor-council cities, we expect to see approximately 208 percent increases in lobbying spending in council-manager cities. This finding is consistent with the aforementioned theoretical argument that city managers are more willing to spend money on lobbying than the elected mayors due to their higher levels of motivation and expertise.

The estimated coefficients of the control variables indicate that public goods gaps, ethnic composition, and financial conditions have substantial effects on intergovernmental lobbying activities, suggesting that some cities invest more in paid representation than others. This variation of investment in hiring professional lobbyists may significantly affect the equity of democratic representation and social resource allocation and further shows the normative importance of studying intergovernmental lobbying (Loftis and Kettler 2015). However, a more detailed analysis of the control variables is beyond the focus of the current research and can be found in the study of Goldstein and You (2017).

Although Tables 2 and 3 provide consistent evidence supporting the effect of executive institutions, there might be empirical concerns about the robustness of the main findings. Two main concerns – measurement error and model misspecification – merit discussion. To address the potential measurement error, I replaced the logged measure of lobbying spending with lobbying spending per capita. As Table 4 shows, executive institutions still have a significantly positive impact on lobbying spending per capita. Substantively, all other things being equal, council-manager cities tend to spend 0.25 more dollars per capita on formally lobbying the federal government than mayor-council cities.

I addressed the potential model misspecification concerns regarding model dependence, pretreatment and posttreatment variables, and heterogeneous effects. To reduce model dependence in parametric causal inference, I used nonparametric propensity score matching (PSM) and inverse probability weighting (IPW) to check the robustness of the main findings (Ho et al. 2007).

Table 3 Determinants of (in) lobbying spending across cities

	Model 3		Model 4	
	Coefficient (Robust SE)	p-value	Coefficient (Robust SE)	p-value
Council-manager	2.333 (0.42)	0.000	2.081 (0.93)	0.026
Public goods gap ($)	0.001 (0.00)	0.552	2.230 (0.42)	0.000
Population (1,000)	19.767 (6.05)	0.001	0.002 (0.00)	0.478
Land area (1,000 sq. miles)	−15.018 (27.93)	0.591	20.008 (6.01)	0.001
Water area (1,000 sq. miles)	−0.357 (0.12)	0.002	−14.861 (27.30)	0.586
Senior (%)	0.483 (0.15)	0.001	−0.368 (0.11)	0.001
Student (%)	13.251 (2.91)	0.000	0.455 (0.15)	0.003
Ethnic heterogeneity	−0.084 (0.03)	0.015	12.177 (2.91)	0.000
Median income ($1,000)	0.208 (0.14)	0.150	−0.084 (0.03)	0.016
Unemployment (%)	−0.304 (0.11)	0.007	0.223 (0.14)	0.119
Households in poverty	58.324 (10.17)	0.000	−0.278 (0.11)	0.013
Gini index	−19.559 (3.57)	0.000	58.899 (10.12)	0.000
Property tax share of revenue	−14.635 (3.23)	0.000	−18.786 (3.59)	0.000
Intergovernmental transfer share of revenue	2.864 (0.94)	0.002	−12.727 (3.36)	0.000
Democrat house representative	4.239 (1.03)	0.000	2.892 (0.94)	0.002
Democrat senator			4.124 (1.02)	0.000

Republican governor	0.883 (0.55)	0.111	0.919 (0.55)	0.096
Year fixed effects	Y		Y	
Constant	−38.995 (5.80)	0.000	−40.509 (5.81)	0.000
Sigma	13.690 (0.30)	0.000	13.660 (0.30)	0.000
Observations	17,626		17,626	
Pseudo R^2	0.066		0.066	
AIC	40,265.247		40,226.686	
BIC	40,506.338		40,475.555	

Note: Two-tailed p-values. Tobit models. The dependent variable is the amount of money (logged) a city spends on lobbying in a year. Models also include year dummies that are not reported. Cluster-robust standard errors are used (clustered at the city level).

Table 4 Determinants of lobbying spending per capita ($) across cities

	Model 5	
	Coefficient (Robust SE)	*p*-value
Council-manager	0.248 (0.10)	0.011
Public goods gap ($)	0.227 (0.05)	0.000
Population (1,000)	−0.000 (0.00)	0.458
Land area (1,000 sq. miles)	1.673 (0.37)	0.000
Water area (1,000 sq. miles)	0.361 (1.66)	0.827
Senior (%)	−0.033 (0.01)	0.009
Student (%)	0.039 (0.02)	0.017
Ethnic heterogeneity	0.979 (0.31)	0.001
Median income ($1,000)	−0.007 (0.00)	0.061
Unemployment (%)	0.030 (0.02)	0.059
Households in poverty	−0.026 (0.01)	0.031
Gini index	5.472 (1.11)	0.000
Property tax share of revenue	−1.762 (0.40)	0.000
Intergovernmental transfer share of revenue	−1.371 (0.36)	0.000
Democrat house representative	0.245 (0.10)	0.012
Democrat senator	0.390 (0.11)	0.001
Republican governor	0.108 (0.06)	0.075
Year fixed effects	Y	
Constant	1.437 (0.07)	0.000
Sigma	−4.049 (0.65)	0.000
Observations	17,626	
Pseudo R^2	0.092	
AIC	22,583.742	
BIC	22,832.610	

Note: Two-tailed *p*-values. Tobit models. The dependent variable is lobbying spending per capita in a year. Models also include year dummies that are not reported. Cluster-robust standard errors are used (clustered at the city level).

As Tables 5 and 6 show, after matching cities with demographic, fiscal, and political factors and year fixed effects, the council-manager institution still has a

Table 5 Average treatment effects of the council-manager executive institution on lobbying participation

	Coef.	Robust SE	z	$P > z$	[95% Conf.	interval]
PSM results	0.059	0.008	7.740	0.000	0.044	0.073
IPW results	0.058	0.006	9.080	0.000	0.0451	0.070

Table 6 Average treatment effects of the council-manager executive institution on (in) lobbying spending

	Coef.	Robust SE	z	P > z	[95% Conf.	interval]
PSM results	0.613	0.081	7.560	0.000	0.454	0.771
IPW results	0.603	0.067	9.030	0.000	0.472	0.734

statistically significant average treatment effect on city lobbying participation and lobbying spending.

Several pretreatment variables may exist and potentially confound the main findings. For instance, the adoption of executive institutions tends to be associated with the reform of legislative institutions or direct democracy, which may also affect policymakers' lobbying decisions (Lubell, Feiock, and De La Cruz 2009). Therefore, I further include these city-level institutions as control variables in Table 7. Although the models in Table 7 provide consistent evidence supporting the effect of executive institutions, legislative institutions or direct democracy show negligible impact on lobbying spending in American cities. Specifically, the coefficients of the percentage of district-based elections and the presence of referendum or recall are not statistically significant. However, the presence of initiative has a statistically significant impact on lobbying participation and spending. Substantively, cities with initiatives are 61 percent more likely than those without initiatives to formally lobby the federal government. Compared to cities without initiatives, we expect to see an approximate 406 percent increase in lobbying spending in cities with initiatives. These results seem to suggest that citizens' power of bypassing their city legislature to make public policy could induce city leaders to invest more money in formally lobbying the federal government for extra resources.

Although the key theoretical argument of this work is about executive institutions of American cities, the specific theoretical mechanisms (e.g., time horizon or policy expertise) occur at the individual level. Executive institutions determine which type of executives are elected or hired and, therefore, individual-level characteristics may serve as the mediators between institutions and lobbying decisions. Unfortunately, to my knowledge, there is no individual-level database covering thousands of executives during the observation period.[4] Given this data limitation, this work could not systematically verify the effects of the main theoretical mechanisms. Nevertheless, I found some compelling evidence to support the main theoretical arguments. First, as mentioned before, previous research using data collected from a small sample of cities suggested that city managers tend to have a longer tenure than city mayors (Ammons and Bosse 2005; McNitt 2010). Thus, city managers may have a longer time horizon and a lower discount rate than city mayors. Second, if the aforementioned expertise argument is correct and some elected mayors work full-time, cities with full-time mayors as government executives would be more likely to participate or invest in lobbying activities than those with part-time mayors as

---

[4] Existing empirical research with individual-level executive information often only has a sample size smaller than 200, such as the studies of McCabe et al. (2008), Zhang and Feiock (2009), or Carreri and Payson (2021).

Table 7 Including other city institutional characteristics

	Model 6 (Logit; DV = Participation)		Model 7 (Tobit; DV = logged spending)	
	Odds ratio (*t*-statistic)	*p*-value	Coefficient (Robust SE)	*p*-value
Council-manager	1.321 (2.00)	0.045	1.591 (0.95)	0.093
District-based elections (%)	1.000 (−0.24)	0.809	−0.003 (0.01)	0.755
Initiative	1.610 (3.63)	0.000	4.059 (0.92)	0.000
Referendum	0.881 (−1.13)	0.257	−1.059 (0.84)	0.208
Recall	1.048 (0.37)	0.711	0.489 (0.96)	0.610
Public goods gap ($)	1.326 (3.90)	0.000	2.225 (0.42)	0.000
Population (1,000)	1.001 (0.55)	0.581	0.001 (0.00)	0.542
Land area (1,000 sq. miles)	20.22 (0.90)	0.366	19.246 (5.91)	0.001
Water area (1,000 sq. miles)	6.650 (0.57)	0.569	−15.301 (26.95)	0.570
Senior (%)	0.956 (−2.78)	0.005	−0.363 (0.11)	0.001
Student (%)	1.050 (2.41)	0.016	0.482 (0.15)	0.001
Ethnic heterogeneity	4.559 (3.17)	0.002	13.007 (2.88)	0.000
Median income ($1,000)	0.991 (−1.89)	0.059	−0.090 (0.03)	0.010
Unemployment (%)	1.034 (1.73)	0.083	0.246 (0.14)	0.085
Households in poverty	0.965 (−2.41)	0.016	−0.305 (0.11)	0.006

Gini index	2,023.0 (5.39)	0.000	60.559 (10.12)	0.000
Property tax share of revenue	0.0971 (−5.02)	0.000	−17.769 (3.55)	0.000
Intergovernmental transfer share of revenue	0.203 (−3.38)	0.001	−10.721 (3.43)	0.002
Democrat house representative	1.491 (2.86)	0.004	2.751 (0.92)	0.003
Democrat senator	1.748 (3.89)	0.000	3.645 (1.02)	0.000
Republican governor	1.129 (1.59)	0.112	0.791 (0.54)	0.145
Year fixed effects	Y		Y	
Constant	0.004 (−6.92)	0.000	−43.449 (5.85)	0.000
Sigma			13.551 (0.30)	0.000
Observations	17,626		17,626	
Pseudo R^2	0.159		0.07	
AIC	16,438.2		40,083.650	
BIC	16,710.4		40,363.627	

Note: Two-tailed *p*-values. Models also include year dummies that are not reported. Cluster-robust standard errors are used (clustered at the city level).

government executives. Further, they would be less likely to participate or invest in lobbying activities than cities with professional executives. I include a new dummy in Table 8, indicating full-time mayors in the models,[5] and the point estimates, although not statistically significant, are consistent with my argument.

Additionally, cities' investments in lobbying the state governments may have a substitutive relationship with their investments in lobbying the federal government due to limited resources. They are not controlled for in my models due to the lack of information. However, this omitted variable should not substantively change the main findings. This is because there is no clear theoretical reason to believe that the pattern of city governments spending money on formally lobbying the state governments is different from that of city governments spending money on formally lobbying the federal government. If executive institutions have the same effect on cities' investments in lobbying the state and federal governments, the potential bias should favor the null hypothesis.

Moreover, in addition to my theoretical analysis on time horizon or policy expertise, an alternative explanation is that mayors may be better connected with federal officials than professional managers. Therefore, given their advantage in informal lobbying, the elected mayors may engage less with formal lobbying. However, there is no systematic evidence in the existing literature to support this argument. In fact, if the direct purpose of lobbying is to provide a legislative subsidy (Hall and Deardorff 2006; Straus 2015), informal lobbying should complement formal lobbying. This is because more politically active local politicians are more likely to need professional lobbyists to monitor policy developments in Washington DC, meet with federal officials and their aides, help formulate politically feasible policy proposals, and testify at congressional committee hearings (Nownes 1999, 2006).[6] Even if federal officials informally support the policy position of local executives, the latter still needs the help of lobbyists who are familiar with federal rules, schedules, and policies to conduct the specific advocacy activities. Federal officials might also need local executives to pay the cost of hiring professionals for parsing policy information and providing policy options. This situation should make it less likely that a statistically significant and positive impact is identified by the empirical models in this section. Therefore, based on this analysis, any bias is expected to work in favor of the null hypothesis.

---

[5] The reference category is cities with part-time mayors as government executives.

[6] In fact, according to AGRP, "What many people regard as lobbying – the actual communication with government officials – represents the smallest portion of a lobbyist's time; a far greater proportion is devoted to the other aspects of preparation, information and communication." http:// grprofessionals.org/about-lobbying/what-is-lobbying

Table 8 The effect of full-time mayors on city lobbying spending

	Model 8 (Logit; DV = Participation)		Model 9 (Tobit; DV = logged spending)	
	Odds ratio (*t*-statistic)	*p*-value	Coefficient (Robust SE)	*p*-value
Council-manager	1.686 (2.94)	0.003	3.644 (1.34)	0.007
Full-time mayor	1.349 (1.41)	0.158	2.459 (1.53)	0.108
Public goods gap ($)	1.322 (3.90)	0.000	2.233 (0.42)	0.000
Population (1,000)	1.001 (0.64)	0.524	0.002 (0.00)	0.518
Land area (1,000 sq. miles)	16.71 (0.96)	0.336	19.575 (5.90)	0.001
Water area (1,000 sq. miles)	10.54 (0.73)	0.463	−13.191 (26.78)	0.622
Senior (%)	0.955 (−2.79)	0.005	−0.377 (0.11)	0.001
Student (%)	1.048 (2.33)	0.020	0.463 (0.15)	0.002
Ethnic heterogeneity	4.103 (2.97)	0.003	12.117 (2.91)	0.000
Median income ($1,000)	0.992 (−1.79)	0.073	−0.081 (0.03)	0.020
Unemployment (%)	1.033 (1.67)	0.095	0.235 (0.14)	0.101
Households in poverty	0.965 (−2.37)	0.018	−0.296 (0.11)	0.009
Gini index	1,554.9 (5.26)	0.000	59.047 (10.12)	0.000
Property tax share of revenue	0.0862 (−5.24)	0.000	−18.958 (3.61)	0.000

Table 8 (cont.)

	Model 8 (Logit; DV = Participation)		Model 9 (Tobit; DV = logged spending)	
	Odds ratio (*t*-statistic)	*p*-value	Coefficient (Robust SE)	*p*-value
Intergovernmental transfer share of revenue	0.162 (−3.99)	0.000	−12.834 (3.36)	0.000
Democrat house representative	1.510 (2.95)	0.003	2.951 (0.94)	0.002
Democrat senator	1.832 (4.27)	0.000	4.114 (1.02)	0.000
Republican governor	1.139 (1.72)	0.085	0.887 (0.55)	0.108
Year fixed effects	Y		Y	
Constant	0.005 (−6.85)	0.000	−42.151 (5.86)	0.000
Sigma			13.645 (0.30)	0.000
Observations	17,626		17,626	
Pseudo R²	0.154		0.067	
AIC	16,527.5		40,207.797	
BIC	16,776.3		40,464.443	

Note: Two-tailed *p*-values. Models also include year dummies that are not reported. Cluster-robust standard errors are used (clustered at the city level).

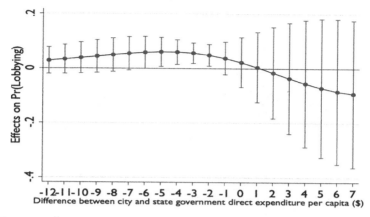

Figure 4 Average marginal effects of executive institutions on lobbying participation as public goods gap changes.

Further, anecdotal evidence suggests that cities lobby through institutional networks, such as the US conference of mayors or ICMA (Jensen 2018). However, it is extremely difficult to collect systematic information on cities' lobbying investments through institutional networks. Therefore, we do not know which type of government executives are more likely to invest in lobbying the federal government through institutional networks.[7] Nevertheless, the phenomenon of lobbying through networks is not likely to challenge the main argument and findings. The careers of professional executives are determined by their reputation in the national labor market, while local elections mainly determine the careers of political executives. Therefore, professional executives should have a stronger incentive to maintain a professional commitment to intergovernmental lobbying. Under these circumstances, we should have more confidence in the statistically significant findings in the main models.

Finally, are the effects of executive institutions conditional on the public demands of local communities? To check this possibility, I tested the potential interaction effect between the council-manager form of government and the public goods gap measured by the difference between city and state government direct expenditure per capita ($) (Goldstein and You 2017). However, as shown in Figures 4 and 5, there is not sufficient evidence to support this interaction effect.

---

[7] Network participation cannot be used as a proxy for lobbying investments through networks because there is little variation in this variable. For instance, the US Conference of Mayors has more than 1,400 city members. ICMA has more than 3,000 city members. These networks' city members have almost covered all cities in the research sample.

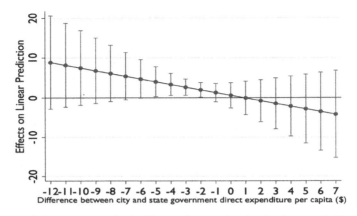

Figure 5 Average marginal effects of executive institutions on lobbying
spending as public goods gap changes.

2.3 Summary

In this section, I used a dataset covering more than 1,200 cities between 1999
and 2012 and a series of models to empirically test the impact of executive
institutions on lobbying participation and lobbying spending among the
American local governments. My estimates exhibited a high correlation
between executive institutions and lobbying participation or lobbying spending.
In this section, I aimed to understand intergovernmental lobbying better through
an actor-level perspective and contribute an institutional dimension to the study
of intergovernmental lobbying.

This section aligns with a recent trend in public administration, public policy,
and political science that seeks to identify the political or policy consequences
of American city institutions (Clingermayer and Feiock 2001; Feiock, Jeong,
and Kim 2003; Krebs and Pelissero 2010; Lubell, Feiock, and De La Cruz 2009;
Trounstine 2010; Trounstine and Valdini 2008). My analysis corroborates that,
in intergovernmental lobbying, what differentiates one government executive
from another is the incentive structure and expertise that support their decisions
regarding each policy issue.

Moreover, numerous social science studies have discussed the effects of
intergovernmental relations on local governance (see Bardhan 2002; Oates
1999; Treisman 2007). However, much less attention is paid to the potential
effects of local governance on intergovernmental relations. The theoretical and
empirical analysis in this section reveals that local institutions may affect
intergovernmental relations by shaping the process of intergovernmental

lobbying. Therefore, future research on the origins of intergovernmental relations should pay more attention to the potential effects of local factors.

The logic of intergovernmental lobbying also has important implications for social equity. The results suggest that the current system might favor council-manager governments and significantly shape the provision of public goods in a society. Therefore, researchers may consider the intergovernmental lobbying determined by local executive institutions when studying political, economic, and social equity across jurisdictions. Practitioners should also pay more attention to institutional variations in the public sector when reforming lobbying regulations in the future.

Local institutions and actor-level motivations and resources on the supply side of public goods deserve more attention in future research on intergovernmental lobbying. My theoretical analysis focuses on the local governments that lobby rather than those that are lobbied. The key hypotheses generated in this research may also apply to the cases of cities lobbying states or cities lobbying cities. Therefore, future research with more fine-grained data can further test the applicability of these results in other types of vertical or horizontal lobbying activities. Moreover, in addition to the institutions mentioned in this section, future research may also theorize and empirically test the effects of other types of local institutional designs on the lobbying activities of local governments.

3 Legislative Professionalism and State Lobbying Activities

3.1 Theoretical Analysis

What determines state governments' participation and investment in lobbying the federal government? State governments spend millions of dollars lobbying the federal government each year. They often have the same lobbying targets, such as the US Senate, the US House of Representatives, and various government departments (Baumgartner et al. 2009). Further, like private organizations, states lobby the federal government for additional resources or policy support. Nevertheless, little research has systematically examined the determinants of state lobbying activities.

This section establishes a theoretical relationship between legislative professionalism and state lobbying activities. Legislative professionalism refers to the overall level of legislative capacity by a state government, measured with a specific set of institutional developments regarding staff or expenditure for the legislature, legislative compensation, and time in sessions (Bowen and Greene 2014). Previous studies have highlighted the influential role of legislative professionalism in shaping state governments' policy adoption or resource allocation (Jansa, Hansen, and Gray 2019; Maestas 2000; Owings and Borck

2000; Shipan and Volden 2006). Besides a measure of legislative capacity (Fortunato and Turner 2018), scholars also view legislative professionalism as a measure of political expertise (Shipan and Volden 2014).

Based on the existing literature, we can thus reasonably expect that a state government with a high level of legislative professionalism uses its resources and expertise when making decisions regarding lobbying the federal government. I argue that legislative professionalism has a positive impact on state lobbying participation or spending through two mechanisms.

First, legislative professionalism motivates state policymakers to allocate resources for lobbying the federal government. Multiple studies have shown that more professionalized legislatures can more effectively collect information from voters and are more responsive to citizen preferences (Berry, Berkman, and Schneiderman 2000; Fortunato and Turner 2018; Maestas 2000; Shipan and Volden 2014). Therefore, more professionalized legislatures can more efficiently translate public opinion into policy outcomes. Median voters tend to have a relatively lower socioeconomic status and higher demands for public goods than political elites (Meltzer and Richard 1981, 1983). Therefore, legislative professionalism could motivate state governments to lobby the federal government for additional resources to meet their demands.

Second, legislative professionalism provides the necessary skills, expertise, or resources for facilitating state lobbying activities. Lobbying generally incurs high transaction costs, including hiring appropriate lobbyists for their political connections or expertise, coordinating with the lobbyists to prepare policy proposals for federal officials, and monitoring their behavior to ensure they deliver the promised service. A highly professionalized state legislature will have more staff, time, and resources to overcome these transaction costs, such as facilitating the hiring of, coordination with, and monitoring of professional lobbyists in Washington. With better access to professional lobbyists in Washington, it is easier for state governments to form policy streams and share their policy ideas or proposals with federal officials (Kingdon 1984).

Therefore, this study has the following hypothesis.

Key Hypothesis: State legislative professionalism increases a state's likelihood of investing resources in formally lobbying the federal government.

3.2 Evidence

I tested the hypotheses with a panel dataset covering fifty states from 1999 to 2011. The state lobbying information is drawn from the website of the Center for Responsive Politics, and the unit of analysis is a state-year. Figure 6 shows

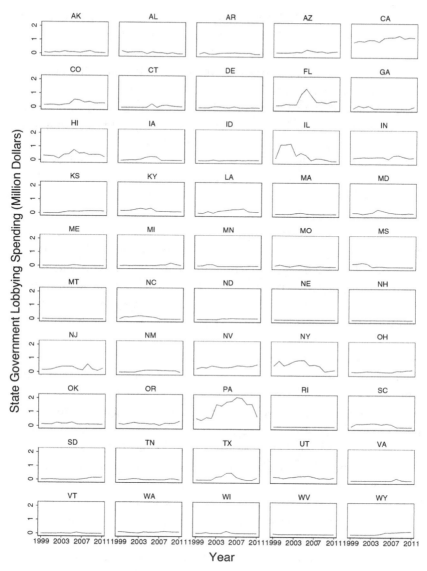

Figure 6 State government lobbying spending (1999–2011).

each state's annual lobbying spending during the observation period. There are two dependent variables of interest. I set the first dependent variable as a dummy equal to 1 if a state government submits a federal lobbying report in a year, and 0 if otherwise. I employed logit models to predict the binary dependent variable. The second dependent variable of interest is the amount a state government invests in lobbying the federal government. It is measured with the natural log of the level of lobbying expense. Given the nonnegative nature of the dependent variable and that the LDA only requires the registration of any organization that contributes more than $10,000 toward lobbying activities each year, I use a tobit model to analyze lobbying spending to deal with the potential censoring problem among states.

The key independent variable is legislative professionalism. Following previous literature (Fortunato and Turner 2018; Squire 2017), I first employed the commonly used Squire Index to test the key hypotheses. The Squire Index was developed to measure the degree to which a state legislature resembles the US Congress along three dimensions (legislators' salaries, days in session, and staff per member) and is theoretically bounded between 0 and 1.

Moreover, professionalism may have multidimensional implications, and some states choose to professionalize some components more than others. Therefore, I also used the two-dimensional indices developed by Bowen and Greene (2014) based on multidimensional scaling (MDS) to measure professionalism. The first dimension (MDS 1) represents the broad differences between amateur and professional legislatures. Conversely, the second dimension (MDS 2) represents the differences between support-intensive (high staff support and short sessions) and work-intensive (low staff support and long sessions) legislatures. Compared to the one-dimensional Squire Index, Bowen and Greene's two-dimensional measures can more comprehensively capture the commonality and variation of legislative professionalism across the states.

As the Squire Index is measured about once a decade and Bowen and Greene's indices (2014) are measured biennially, I inputted the missing values with the observable values in the previous year (Fortunato and Turner 2018). If the Squire Index, MDS 1, and MDS 2 have a consistently positive impact on state lobbying participation and lobbying expenses, then there is strong evidence that legislature professionalism increases state lobbying activities.

State policymakers' lobbying activities are also likely to be influenced by other factors. Building on previous research on state politics (Berry and Berry 1990; Shipan and Volden 2006), I included political, financial, and demographic controls in the models. As one of the most important goals of state politicians is to be reelected, researchers argue that the proximity of state elections is correlated with the probability of adopting a new policy (Besley and Coate 2003; Nicholson-Crotty 2015). Therefore, I include a dummy variable indicating a gubernatorial election year in the models. The gubernatorial election information is collected from the Governors Dataset created by Carl Klarner.[8]

---

[8] Klarner, Carl. 2013. "Governors Dataset." https://hdl.handle.net/1902.1/20408, Harvard Dataverse.

Political scientists have also proposed partisan and ideological explanations for state government spending (Nicholson-Crotty 2015). The partisan theory suggests that the governing party spends money on policies that satisfy core constituencies. As the core supporters and members of the Democratic Party are assumed to prefer the expansion of public service, I expect that state lobbying spending increases with state elite liberalism. Specifically, I set a dummy equal to 1 if a governor was a Democrat, and 0 otherwise. I also included a measure of government liberal ideology drawn from the study of Berry et al. (2010) in the models.[9] Conversely, the electoral theory suggests that politicians are likely to manipulate government spending to buy the median votes. Accordingly, I also included a measure of citizen liberal ideology drawn from the study of Berry et al. (2010) in the models.

The financial characteristics of state governments may also affect their lobbying spending. For instance, the size of government expenditure, fiscal health,[10] the percentage of federal transfer, and the percentage of debt burden may have a directly stimulating or dampening effect on state governments' lobbying spending. The information on these variables is collected from The Government Finance Database (Pierson, Hand, and Thompson 2015).[11]

Similarly, demographic characteristics can potentially affect the resources or motivations of state governments, thus shaping their lobbying spending. I included the per capita personal income, rate of unemployment, and population size in the models, as these variables are most likely to be correlated with the demands of public goods in each state. The data are collected from the websites of the Bureau of Economic Analysis[12] and the Bureau of Labor Statistics[13]. I also included year fixed effects in logit and tobit models to capture any time-specific trend. I did not include state fixed effects in the models, given that the measures of legislature professionalism were stable during the observed period, and including state fixed effects in the models would lead to an unconverged estimation process. Further, stable political controls should also help isolate the effects of legislative professionalism. The summary statistics of all variables are shown in Table 9.

---

[9] Richard C. Fording. 2018. "State Ideology Data." https://rcfording.wordpress.com/state-ideol ogy-data/

[10] This measure is calculated using the following formula: $\frac{(Total\ revenue - Total\ expenditure)}{Total\ expenditure}$ (Berry and Berry 1990).

[11] Kawika Pierson, Michael L. Hand, and Thompson. "The Government Finance Database." http:// willamette.edu/mba/research-impact/public-datasets/index.html

[12] Bureau of Economic Analysis. "Regional Economic Accounts: Download." https://apps.bea .gov/regional/downloadzip.cfm

[13] Bureau of Labor Statistics. "Civilian Noninstitutional Population and Associated Rate and Ratio Measures for Model-Based Areas." www.bls.gov/lau/rdscnp16.htm

Table 9 Summary statistics

Variable	Obs.	Mean	Std. Dev.	Min.	Max.
State lobbying participation	650	0.67	0.47	0.00	1.00
State lobbying spending logged	650	8.01	5.68	0.00	14.56
Squire Index	650	0.19	0.11	0.03	0.63
MDS 1	650	0.15	1.65	−1.85	8.58
MDS 2	650	0.13	0.75	−3.07	3.17
Gubernatorial election year	650	0.25	0.43	0.00	1.00
Democrat governor	650	0.46	0.50	0.00	1.00
Government liberal ideology	650	47.53	14.27	17.51	73.62
Citizen liberal ideology	650	51.71	15.80	8.45	95.97
Total expenditure ($1,000)	650	30,140.35	37,195.94	2,271.67	285,238.10
Fiscal health	650	0.04	0.18	−0.76	1.25

Federal transfer (%)	650	26.72	8.09	12.32	101.18
Debt burden (%)	650	55.41	30.98	13.83	245.51
Per capita personal income ($1,000)	650	34.84	7.04	20.73	63.77
Unemployment (%)	650	5.61	2.09	2.30	13.70
Population (1,000)	650	5,901.77	6,484.42	491.78	37,672.65

Table 10 shows the estimates of the determinants of lobbying participation across American states. Given the logit model specifications, the odds ratio for one unit increase in each independent variable and t-statistics in parentheses are provided. The two-tailed p-values are shown in separate columns. Table 10 also reports McFadden R^2 (McFadden 1974), the AIC (Akaike 1974), and the BIC (Schwarz 1978). Further, Table 10 presents specifications with controls only, alongside specifications that include Squire Index or MDS indices. The measures of state legislative professionalism markedly improve model fit, indicating that state lobbying participation varies significantly according to the level of legislative professionalism.

The results in Table 10 strongly support the key hypothesis in this section. After controlling for political, financial, and demographic characteristics, the Squire Index and MDS indices still significantly predict the likelihood a state lobbies the federal government. To interpret and compare the coefficients, I report the percentage change of odds ratio for one standard deviation increase in each variable in Table 11. When all else is equal, when the measures of legislative professionalism of a state increase by one standard deviation, the state is at least 210 percent more likely to lobby the federal government. The odds ratio of one unit increase in the Squire Index in Table 10 seems extremely large. However, as Table 11 shows, the percentage change of odds ratio for one standard deviation increase in the Squire Index is only 220.4 percent. As a robustness check, I ran a Firth logit model (Rainey 2016) and produced similar results (not reported here). Nevertheless, Table 10 does not provide strong evidence to confirm the effects of the control variables.

Table 12 shows the estimated determinants of state lobbying spending. Given the Tobit model specifications, the coefficients for one unit increase in each independent variable and robust standard errors clustered by each state in parentheses are provided. The two-tailed p-values are shown in separate columns. Table III-4 also reports McFadden R^2, AIC, and BIC. I ran three regressions. Model 4 includes all control variables, whereas Models 5 and 6 include the Squire Index and MDS indices, separately. The measures of goodness of fit in Table 12 suggest that legislative professionalism markedly improved model fit.

The results in Table 12 corroborate that, after controlling for political, financial, and demographic factors, legislative professionalism still significantly predicted state lobbying spending. To facilitate the interpretation and comparison of coefficients, I reported the percentage change of state lobbying spending for one standard deviation increase in each independent variable in Table 13. Substantively, the coefficients of the Squire Index and MDS indices indicate that one standard deviation increase in legislative professionalism leads to at least a 128.9 percent increase in state lobbying spending. This result is

Table 10 State legislative professionalism and lobbying participation

	Model 1		Model 2		Model 3	
	Odds ratio (*t*-statistic)	*p*-value	Odds ratio (*t*-statistic)	*p*-value	Odds ratio (*t*-statistic)	*p*-value
Squire Index			25445.5 (2.28)	0.022		
MDS 1					5.291 (3.67)	0.000
MDS 2					4.505 (4.09)	0.000
Gubernatorial election year	0.949 (−0.21)	0.832	1.028 (0.12)	0.906	1.076 (0.29)	0.771
Democrat governor	1.729 (0.95)	0.342	1.988 (1.25)	0.212	2.407 (1.46)	0.143
Government liberal ideology	0.983 (−0.73)	0.466	0.977 (−0.99)	0.321	0.972 (−1.24)	0.214
Citizen liberal ideology	0.985 (−0.89)	0.372	0.978 (−1.16)	0.245	0.978 (−1.13)	0.258
Total expenditure ($1,000)	1.000 (1.99)	0.047	1.000 (0.72)	0.473	1.000 (0.32)	0.751

Table 10 (cont.)

	Model 1		Model 2		Model 3	
	Odds ratio (t-statistic)	p-value	Odds ratio (t-statistic)	p-value	Odds ratio (t-statistic)	p-value
Fiscal health	0.0727	0.087	0.0865	0.142	0.133	0.197
	(-1.71)		(-1.47)		(-1.29)	
Federal transfer (%)	0.948	0.169	0.965	0.269	0.990	0.777
	(-1.38)		(-1.10)		(-0.28)	
Debt burden (%)	0.987	0.230	0.985	0.184	0.991	0.321
	(-1.20)		(-1.33)		(-0.99)	
Per capita personal income ($1,000)	1.033	0.458	1.021	0.662	0.983	0.751
	(0.74)		(0.44)		(-0.32)	
Unemployment (%)	1.204	0.321	1.177	0.429	1.052	0.819
	(0.99)		(0.79)		(0.23)	
Population (1,000)	1.000	0.198	1.000	0.335	1.000	0.103
	(-1.29)		(-0.96)		(-1.63)	
Year fixed effects	Y		Y		Y	
Constant	9.124	0.265	4.998	0.432	142.1	0.042
	(1.11)		(0.79)		(2.03)	

Observations	650	650	650
Pseudo R^2	0.131	0.174	0.234
AIC	763.5	730.4	683.0
BIC	870.9	842.3	799.4

Note: Two-tailed *p*-values. Logit models. The dependent variable is a dummy equal to 1 if a state submits a lobbying report in a year, and 0 otherwise. Models also include year dummies that are not reported. Cluster-robust standard errors are used (clustered at the state level).

Table 11 The percentage change of odds ratio for one standard deviation increase in each variable (Logit models in Table 10)

	Model 1	Model 2	Model 3
Squire Index		220.4	
MDS 1			1,456.2
MDS 2			210.8
Gubernatorial election year	−2.3	1.2	3.2
Democrat governor	31.2	40.5	54.5
Government liberal ideology	−21.6	−28.2	−33.8
Citizen liberal ideology	−21.2	−29.5	−30
Total expenditure ($1,000)	666.8	82.3	40
Fiscal health	−37.5	−35.5	−30.4
Federal transfer (%)	−35.2	−25.3	−7.6
Debt burden (%)	−32.9	−37.4	−25.2
Per capita personal income ($1,000)	25.9	15.4	−11.4
Unemployment (%)	47.3	40.4	11.2
Population (1,000)	−64.7	−46	−67.4

consistent with the theoretical analysis that legislative professionalism increases state lobbying spending motivation and resources. Further, there is consistent evidence that state fiscal health negatively impacts lobbying spending. Again, most control variables show statistically insignificant impacts on the outcome variable.

One potential concern is that there might be endogeneity between expenditures and state legislative professionalism. For instance, Fiorina and Noll (1978a, 1978b) argue that legislatures may professionalize in response to increased duties induced by more lavish government spending. Malhorta (2006) provides empirical support for this argument with an instrumental

Table 12 State legislative professionalism and (in) lobbying spending

	Model 4		Model 5		Model 6	
	Coefficient (Robust SE)	p-value	Coefficient (Robust SE)	p-value	Coefficient (Robust SE)	p-value
Squire Index			26.185 (9.88)	0.008		
MDS 1					2.654 (0.82)	0.001
MDS 2					1.711 (0.78)	0.029
Gubernatorial election year	−0.249 (0.85)	0.770	−0.062 (0.80)	0.938	−0.080 (0.80)	0.921
Democrat governor	2.251 (2.18)	0.303	1.979 (2.12)	0.352	2.522 (2.10)	0.230
Government liberal ideology	−0.068 (0.08)	0.412	−0.062 (0.08)	0.452	−0.084 (0.08)	0.305
Citizen liberal ideology	−0.064 (0.07)	0.349	−0.090 (0.07)	0.178	−0.076 (0.07)	0.256
Total expenditure ($1,000)	0.000 (0.00)	0.340	−0.000 (0.00)	0.706	−0.000 (0.00)	0.272
Fiscal health	−11.936 (5.62)	0.034	−10.994 (5.31)	0.039	−10.403 (5.11)	0.042
Federal transfer (%)	−0.202 (0.13)	0.122	−0.152 (0.13)	0.227	−0.115 (0.12)	0.337

Table 12 (cont.)

	Model 4		Model 5		Model 6	
	Coefficient (Robust SE)	p-value	Coefficient (Robust SE)	p-value	Coefficient (Robust SE)	p-value
Debt burden (%)	−0.048 (0.04)	0.250	−0.056 (0.04)	0.166	−0.045 (0.04)	0.222
Per capita personal income ($1,000)	0.196 (0.17)	0.259	0.156 (0.17)	0.362	0.122 (0.17)	0.479
Unemployment (%)	0.884 (0.63)	0.162	0.704 (0.63)	0.263	0.615 (0.60)	0.310
Population (1,000)	−0.000 (0.00)	0.978	0.000 (0.00)	0.994	−0.000 (0.00)	0.726
Year fixed effects	Y		Y		Y	
Constant	9.591 (7.55)	0.204	7.996 (7.65)	0.296	13.697 (7.17)	0.057
Sigma	7.332 (0.68)	0.000	7.134 (0.67)	0.000	7.030 (0.66)	0.000
Observations	650		650		650	
Pseudo R^2	0.034		0.043		0.047	
AIC	3,426.567		3,395.430		3,384.340	
BIC	3,538.491		3,511.831		3,505.218	

Note: Two-tailed p-values. Tobit models. The dependent variable is the amount (logged) a state spends on lobbying in a year. Models also include year dummies that are not reported. Cluster-robust standard errors are used (clustered at the state level).

Table 13 The percentage change of lobbying spending for one standard deviation increase in each variable (Tobit models in Table 12)

	Model 4	**Model 5**	**Model 6**
Squire Index		300.6	
MDS 1			437.3
MDS 2			128.9
Gubernatorial election year	−10.8	−2.7	−3.4
Democrat governor	111.5	98	124.9
Government liberal ideology	−97.3	−89	−119.4
Citizen liberal ideology	−101.3	−141.8	−119.4
Total expenditure ($1,000)	165.8	−55.5	−193.4
Fiscal health	−213.8	−196.9	−186.4
Federal transfer (%)	−163.4	−123.1	−93.2
Debt burden (%)	−147.5	−172.4	−139.3
Per capita personal income ($1,000)	137.7	109.9	86.1
Unemployment (%)	184.3	146.8	128.2
Population (1,000)	−5	1.2	−45.8

variable design. Nevertheless, arguably, the instruments for spending in Malhorta (2006) (i.e., the number of state legislators, per capita revenue from the federal government, and per capita mineral revenues) still could shape state legislative professionalism by directly changing political dynamics or inducing more duties, thus violating the exclusion restriction assumption.

This work attempts to address this potential endogeneity concern in two ways. First, it included the most commonly recognized antecedents of state profession-alism in the models as control variables, including total expenditure (Malhorta 2006), population (Squire and Hamm 2005), and ideology (King 2000; Mooney 1995). Second, as mentioned before, the Squire Index is measured about once a decade, and Bowen and Greene's MDS indices are measured biennially. Thus, in Table 14, I used MDS 1 and 2, lagged by two years, as the explanatory variables. The results remain consistent with the main findings. Ideally, this work could develop an instrument variable design to test the causal effect of legislative professionalism on lobbying participation or spending. However, I could not identify an exogenous variable that affects state legislative professionalism and does not affect state lobbying activities in the observation period. In other words, it is difficult to find a valid instrument variable that satisfies the exclusion restriction assumption. Therefore, I encourage future research with more refined designs, such as natural experiments, to further verify the main hypothesis in this section.

Another concern is that the outliers may significantly bias the estimated results. For instance, California and Pennsylvania lobbied the federal government every year, and these two states spent the biggest amount of money on lobbying during the observation period. Further, these two states have a high level of legislative professionalism. Therefore, I account for the effects of these outliers by including them as two dummy variables (CA and PA) in the statistical models. Table 15 reports the logit models of lobbying participation. As CA and PA predict lobbying participation perfectly, twenty-six observations are automatically dropped from the logit models. Table 16 reports the tobit models with CA and PA as additional controls. Tables 15 and 16 show that legislative professionalism has a statistically significant and positive impact on lobbying participation and spending after accounting for the outliers. The point estimates are similar to those reported in Tables 10 and 12.

3.3 Summary

This section examines how legislative professionalism affects state governments' decisions regarding lobbying the federal government. The theoretical analysis shows that states with a higher level of legislative professionalism have stronger motivations to meet the demands of the median voters and more resources to overcome the transaction cost involved in the formal lobbying process. Therefore, legislative professionalism should positively impact state lobbying participation and spending. The analysis of the panel dataset covering fifty states from 1999 to 2011 provides consistent empirical support for the key arguments.

This section has important implications for the literature of state politics, lobbying, and intergovernmental relations. There is a lack of state politics research that quantitatively examines the lobbying activities of state governments, which are commonly viewed as important means for subnational governments to obtain resources from the national government (Jensen 2018).

Table 14 Determinants of state lobbying participation and (in) spending (MDS lagged by two years)

	Model 7 (Logit)		Model 8 (Tobit)	
	Coefficient (Robust SE)	*p*-value	Coefficient (Robust SE)	*p*-value
L2.MDS 1	5.059 (3.28)	0.001	2.663 (0.45)	0.000
L2.MDS 2	4.830 (4.08)	0.000	1.959 (0.50)	0.000
Gubernatorial election year	1.024 (0.10)	0.922	−0.228 (0.94)	0.807
Democrat governor	1.859 (0.98)	0.328	1.817 (1.09)	0.097
Government liberal ideology	0.974 (−1.10)	0.272	−0.070 (0.05)	0.134
Citizen liberal ideology	0.975 (−1.13)	0.259	−0.090 (0.03)	0.009
Total expenditure ($1,000)	1.000 (0.33)	0.744	−0.000 (0.00)	0.127
Fiscal health	0.147 (−1.02)	0.307	−9.529 (3.68)	0.010
Federal transfer (%)	0.990 (−0.33)	0.744	−0.104 (0.06)	0.095
Debt burden (%)	0.991 (−0.90)	0.366	−0.040 (0.02)	0.015
Per capita personal income ($1,000)	0.996 (−0.08)	0.936	0.149 (0.09)	0.093
Unemployment (%)	1.048 (0.22)	0.826	0.546 (0.28)	0.050

Table 14 (cont.)

	Model 7 (Logit)		Model 8 (Tobit)	
	Coefficient (Robust SE)	*p*-value	Coefficient (Robust SE)	*p*-value
Population (1,000)	1.000 (–1.56)	0.118	–0.000 (0.00)	0.719
Year fixed effects	Y		Y	
Constant	98.87 (1.83)	0.067	12.156 (4.14)	0.003
Observations	550		550	
Pseudo R^2	0.225		0.045	
AIC	583.6		2,889.223	
BIC	687.0		2,996.971	

Note: Two-tailed *p*-values. Models also include year dummies that are not reported. Cluster-robust standard errors are used (clustered at the state level). L2: lagged by two years.

Table 15 Determinants of state lobbying participation (excluding CA and PA)

	Model 9		Model 10	
	Odds Ratio (*t*-statistic)	*p*-value	Odds Ratio (*t*-statistic)	*p*-value
Squire Index	19,404.7 (2.22)	0.026		
MDS 1			5.276 (3.65)	0.000
MDS 2			4.490 (4.06)	0.000
Gubernatorial election year	1.026 (0.11)	0.911	1.075 (0.29)	0.772
Democrat governor	1.946 (1.21)	0.226	2.404 (1.46)	0.144
Government liberal ideology	0.978 (−0.95)	0.343	0.972 (−1.24)	0.215
Citizen liberal ideology	0.978 (−1.20)	0.231	0.978 (−1.13)	0.257
Total expenditure ($1,000)	1.000 (0.62)	0.535	1.000 (0.32)	0.751
Fiscal health	0.0884 (−1.47)	0.141	0.133 (−1.29)	0.197
Federal transfer (%)	0.964 (−1.12)	0.262	0.990 (−0.29)	0.775
Debt burden (%)	0.985 (−1.31)	0.189	0.991 (−0.99)	0.321
Per capita personal income ($1,000)	1.022 (0.46)	0.646	0.983 (−0.32)	0.752

Table 15 (cont.)

	Model 9		Model 10	
	Odds Ratio (*t*-statistic)	*p*-value	Odds Ratio (*t*-statistic)	*p*-value
Unemployment (%)	1.183 (0.82)	0.410	1.053 (0.23)	0.819
Population (1,000)	1.000 (−0.89)	0.372	1.000 (−1.63)	0.103
Year fixed effects	Y		Y	
Constant	4.747 (0.76)	0.445	141.3 (2.03)	0.042
Observations	624		624	
Pseudo R²	0.154		0.214	
AIC	728.5		683.0	
BIC	839.4		798.3	

Note: Two-tailed *p*-values. Logit models. The dependent variable is a dummy equal to 1 if a state submits a lobbying report in a year, and 0 otherwise. Models also include year dummies that are not reported. Cluster-robust standard errors are used (clustered at the state level).

Table 16 Determinants of (in) state lobbying spending (including CA and PA as dummies)

	Model 11		Model 12	
	Coefficient (Robust SE)	*p*-value	Coefficient (Robust SE)	*p*-value
Squire Index	25.608 (9.95)	0.010		
MDS 1			3.636 (1.01)	0.000
MDS 2			3.146 (0.88)	0.000
Gubernatorial election year	−0.036 (0.80)	0.964	0.041 (0.78)	0.958
Democrat governor	1.484 (2.15)	0.490	2.110 (2.07)	0.308
Government liberal ideology	−0.038 (0.08)	0.658	−0.055 (0.08)	0.496
Citizen liberal ideology	−0.103 (0.07)	0.122	−0.094 (0.06)	0.139
Total expenditure ($1,000)	0.000 (0.00)	0.864	−0.000 (0.00)	0.666
Fiscal health	−10.229 (5.32)	0.055	−9.132 (4.94)	0.065
Federal transfer (%)	−0.161 (0.13)	0.203	−0.098 (0.11)	0.396
Debt burden (%)	−0.053 (0.04)	0.190	−0.041 (0.03)	0.233
Per capita personal income ($1,000)	0.130 (0.17)	0.445	0.019 (0.18)	0.914

Table 16 (cont.)

	Model 11		Model 12	
	Coefficient (Robust SE)	p-value	Coefficient (Robust SE)	p-value
Unemployment (%)	0.645 (0.63)	0.306	0.285 (0.61)	0.639
Population (1,000)	−0.000 (0.00)	0.945	−0.000 (0.00)	0.228
CA	−5.780 (3.19)	0.070	−18.177 (4.48)	0.000
PA	2.274 (1.12)	0.042	−5.210 (2.42)	0.032
Year fixed effects	Y		Y	
Constant	8.489 (7.64)	0.267	17.295 (7.29)	0.018
Sigma	7.098 (0.67)	0.000	6.871 (0.66)	0.000
Observations	650		650	
Pseudo R^2	0.045		0.055	
AIC	3,389.872		3,356.461	
BIC	3,506.273		3,477.339	

Note: Two-tailed p-values. Tobit models. The dependent variable the amount of money (logged) a state spends on lobbying in a year. Models also include year dummies that are not reported. Cluster-robust standard errors are used (clustered at the state level).

Federalism literature reveals how state governments make strategic choices to influence resource allocation of the federal government (Nicholson-Crotty 2015). However, it misses state lobbying activities, which are an important link between state politics and federal resource allocation. This section shows that the institutional logic of legislative professionalism identified in the existing literature also applies to state governments' lobbying activities. Future research could build on this work to further explore the effects of other potential determinants of state lobbying activities.

This research also has important practical implications. The financial recessions in recent years, the aging population trend, and the 2019 coronavirus disease (COVID-19) pandemic led to an increase in state and local expenditures on Medicaid, Medicare, and retirement benefits and a decrease in spending on transportation, education, and other public services (Kiewiet and McCubbins 2014; Nicholson-Crotty 2015; Rocco, Béland, and Waddan 2020). State governments have to pursue additional resources from the federal government to satisfy the demands of public goods in their jurisdictions. Hence, the dynamics behind each state's investment in lobbying the federal government could help us understand which states will become the winners or losers in the "new fiscal ice age" (Kiewiet and McCubbins 2014).

4 Bottom-Up Federalism of Lobbying Investment

4.1 Theoretical Analysis

Hundreds of local- and state-level governments invest millions of dollars in hiring professional lobbyists to influence the federal government each year. Given that presumably, both local- and state-level governments are hiring professional lobbyists to obtain resources from and influence policies in the federal government, some interesting questions arise. Do local lobbying activities affect state-level lobbying activities? When local governments within states increase their investments, will the state governments increase or decrease their investments in lobbying the federal government?

This section borrows the concept of bottom-up federalism from research on policy diffusion to explain the vertical policy interactions in intergovernmental lobbying activities in the United States. Policy diffusion refers to the process whereby the policy choice of one government is influenced by that of another (Shipan and Volden 2012; Graham, Shipan, and Volden 2013). Studies have examined the two main categories of horizontal and vertical diffusion processes. Horizontal policy diffusion processes, such as learning, competition, and imitation, received the most attention in previous literature (Gilardi 2010; Gray 1973, 1994; Shipan and Volden 2008; Volden 2006; Walker 1969).

Vertical dynamics in the subnational policy process, such as the coercion mechanism and bottom-up and top-down federalism (Karch 2007, 2012; Karch and Rosenthal 2016; McCann, Shipan, and Volden 2015; Shipan and Volden 2006), have also drawn increased attention from scholars in recent years. However, most previous studies investigate regulatory policy cases, which deal with the interactions between governments and citizens. Nevertheless, besides citizens in their jurisdictions, governments also need to make policy decisions to interact with other governments. We still know little about the following question: Do decisions of intergovernmental interactions diffuse across governments?

This section focuses on the potential effects of local governments' decisions of lobbying the federal government on state governments' corresponding decisions using the case of intergovernmental lobbying. I borrow Shipan and Volden's (2006) policy diffusion theory of bottom-up federalism to analyze the theoretical relationship between local and state lobbying spending. Shipan and Volden (2006) point out that most existing knowledge about intergovernmental policy dependency is about state-to-state diffusion; little is known about the bottom-up diffusion of policies from local to state governments. They argue that policy-oriented learning and interlocality economic or budgetary spillovers can lead state governments to change existing policies. Using the case of anti-smoking laws, Shipan and Volden (2006) provide evidence that policies bubble up from city governments to state governments.

This section brings together intergovernmental lobbying and policy diffusion literature and argues that bottom-up federalism also applies to intergovernmental lobbying. I show that intense lobbying by local governments may have two distinct effects on state governments lobbying the federal government: the snowball effect and the pressure valve effect (Shipan and Volden 2006).

There are three possible sources of the snowball effect. First, increased local lobbying makes this policy tool more salient to state-level policymakers, which increases state lobbying spending. Recent research suggests that states draw policy experience and knowledge within each policy area from local governments (Shipan and Volden 2006, 2014). Moreover, previous research suggests that lobbying can generate substantial returns. For instance, 1 dollar spent on lobbying produces more than 8 dollars in the education sector (De Figueiredo 2006), 1.3 dollars in the energy sector (Kang 2016), 12 dollars in the stock market (Borisov, Goldman, and Gupta 2016), and 40 dollars for city governments (Goldstein and You 2017). Given this potential profitability, a higher level of local investment in lobbying the federal government is more likely to attract the attention of state-level policymakers and lead them to invest more money in lobbying the federal government.

Second, local lobbying activities can result in negative externalities among local governments. For instance, one local government's lobbying investment may reduce a nearby city's likelihood of obtaining the same resources (e.g., earmark or grant) from the federal government. As Payson (2020b) suggests, the benefits of intergovernmental lobbying are positively associated with the own-source revenue per capita of cities. Increased spending by local governments on lobbying the federal government may lead to an unequal distribution of resources within a state. Therefore, state governments may internalize this externality by increasing their own lobbying spending and directly pursuing resources from the federal government to meet the demands of local interest groups and voters.

A third source of the snowball effect is the unaligned political incentives of state and local policymakers. Given different constituencies, state and local policymakers may simultaneously pursue the same limited resources from the federal government to meet the demands of their separate core supporters (Barber and Dynes 2019). As Jensen (2016) points out, state governments also often compete with local governments for federal funding. The result may be an arms race of lobbying investments between state and local policymakers' interests that is adversarial rather than collaborative.

Snowball Effect Hypothesis: The intensity of local lobbying spending is positively associated with that of state lobby spending.

However, as Shipan and Volden (2006) suggest, local policy actions may also produce an opposite effect – the pressure valve effect – on state-level policymakers. Specifically, local lobbying actions may decrease state lobbying spending by reducing the policy pressure on state-level policymakers. If local lobbying spending can help local governments successfully pursue additional resources from the federal government and provide local communities with more public goods (Goldstein and You 2017; Payson 2020b), local policy issues may become less acute. Further, local voters and groups have fewer incentives to advocate for further actions at the state level. Meanwhile, state-level policymakers will feel less policy pressure to respond to local demands. Therefore, state-level policymakers will be less likely to directly respond to their local supporters by allocating resources for lobbying the federal government.

Pressure Valve Effect Hypothesis: The intensity of local lobbying spending is negatively associated with that of state lobby spending.

The snowball and pressure valve effect hypotheses have competing theoretical explanations. To empirically examine which one dominates in the bottom-up federalism of intergovernmental lobbying, I employ empirical data drawn from multiple sources to conduct hypothesis testing.

4.2 Evidence

This section examines the bottom-up federalism of intergovernmental lobbying activities by focusing on the lobbying spending of state and local governments from 1999 to 2011. The dependent variable is the amount of money ($1,000) each state government spends lobbying the federal government each year. The independent variable is the sum of lobbying spending ($1,000) by all city, town, and county governments within a state in a year. Another potential measure of local lobbying activity is the proportion of state populations with local governments lobbying the federal government (Shipan and Volden 2006). However, intergovernmental lobbying is not a regulatory policy that aims to change citizens' behavior directly. The geographic area of towns, cities, and counties may overlap, and, therefore, this potential measure cannot reflect the scale of the overall local lobbying investment. Moreover, an empirical difficulty is that the annual population information for small cities and towns is less available and may be less reliable (Shipan and Volden 2008). Given these reasons, I do not measure the state lobbying activities as a dummy indicating each state's participation in lobbying the federal government to maintain the measurement consistency of the independent and dependent variables. Nevertheless, a logit model with year fixed effects (not reported) does show that local lobbying spending has a statistically significant effect on states' participation in lobbying the federal government. Further, the measure of the independent variables only includes the lobbying information of local general-purpose governments. It does not include the lobbying information of special districts, school districts, or public hospitals. This is because these institutions may not have the same theorized effects as the general-purpose governments, and their lobbying information is much more difficult to identify or collect.

Admittedly, local and state governments may lobby for different policy issues at the federal level. Nevertheless, if we assume that policymakers are motivated by reelection or reappointment, then the state- and local-level governments' purpose in lobbying the federal government should be the same: obtaining more resources or policy support from the federal government to meet supporters' demands. Even if a state government lobbies the federal government for policy support for a state-level policy issue different from local policy issues, the returns of lobbying should still serve the same purpose of improving the quality or quantity of public goods. Local lobbying can still increase or decrease demand for lobbying among state policymakers. Therefore, although I do not have information on issue-specific lobbying spending for each level of government,[14] the potential difference of lobbying issues should not affect the theoretical or empirical inferences.

---

[14] It is hard to collect information on issue-specific lobbying spending because the number and types of policy issues are inconsistent across lobbying reports. I cannot directly identify the

State lobbying investment is also likely to be influenced by other factors that we need to control for. Consistent with the empirical models in Section 3, I included political, financial, and demographic controls. I also used the two-dimensional indices developed by Bowen and Greene (2014) based on MDS to measure legislative professionalism. Given the dynamic and continuous nature of the dependent and independent variables, I employed the Arellano–Bond dynamic model, using current and past information to predict state lobbying spending. This generalized method of moments (GMM) approach first uses differencing to remove the unobserved panel-level effects and then uses instruments (the lagged dependent variable and endogenous variables) to produce moment conditions (Arellano and Bond 1991). A test for the serial correlation structure rejects no autocorrelation of order 1 ($z = -2.34$) and cannot reject no autocorrelation of order 2 ($z = 0.60$). Accordingly, there is evidence that the Arellano–Bond model assumptions are satisfied.

To demonstrate the relationship between local and state lobbying spending in each state from 1999 to 2011, I first calculated a prediction from a linear regression of state lobbying spending and plotted the resulting line, along with a 95 percent confidence interval in Figure 7. The results reveal that there is a positive correlation across most states. Next, I conducted regressions to examine the robustness of these relationships further.

Table 17 presents the Arellano–Bond dynamic panel-data estimation of state lobbying spending. The coefficients, robust standard errors, and two-tailed p-values are reported. I ran two regressions. Model 1 includes only the lagged dependent variable and the variables that capture the political, financial, and demographic characteristics of each state. In Model 2, the key independent variable – local lobbying spending – is added.

The results shown in Table 17 suggest that local lobbying spending has a statistically significant impact on state lobbying spending. When local lobbying spending within a state increases by $1,000, the state lobbying spending increases by $69. This positive effect is statistically significant ($p < 0.05$) after controlling for multiple political, financial, and demographic variables and serial correlation. Therefore, the results shown in Table 16 support the snowball effect in intergovernmental lobbying activities hypothesis.

The control variables also showed some interesting results. Table 17 shows that when a state government increases its total expenditure by $1,000, it will decrease its lobbying spending by $6. This result suggests that governments with a higher level of total expenditure might have fewer resources to lobby the federal government. A 1 percent increase in the federal transfer was associated

---

specific amount of lobbying spending assigned to each issue. This fact makes it difficult to consistently calculate a government's issue-specific lobbying spending or compare two different governments' lobbying spending in a specific policy area in a year.

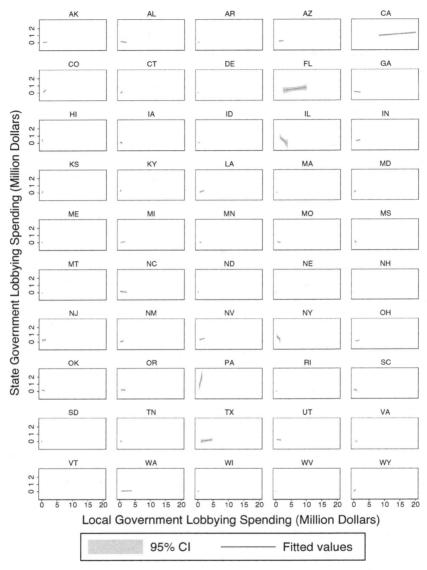

Figure 7 Linear prediction of bottom-up federalism in intergovernmental lobbying.

with a $3,566 increase in state lobbying spending. This result suggests state governments that receive more federal transfers might be more actively seeking to obtain additional resources from the federal government. A 1 percent increase in debt burden was associated with a $2,345 decrease in state lobbying spending. A 1 percent increase in the unemployment rate was associated with a $7,221 increase in state lobbying spending.

Table 17 Arellano–Bond dynamic panel-data estimation of state lobbying spending

	Model 1		Model 2	
	Coefficient (Robust SE)	Two-tailed *p*-value	Coefficient (Robust SE)	Two-tailed *p*-value
Local lobbying spending ($1,000)			0.069 (0.03)	0.031
Lagged state lobbying spending ($1,000)	0.683 (0.06)	0.000	0.657 (0.06)	0.000
MDS 1	55.869 (73.80)	0.449	47.598 (68.91)	0.490
MDS 2	14.482 (54.68)	0.791	11.083 (51.76)	0.830
Gubernatorial election year	−10.418 (8.04)	0.195	−11.151 (7.60)	0.143
Democrat governor	−19.293 (53.59)	0.719	−3.071 (54.52)	0.955
Government liberal ideology	1.423 (1.91)	0.456	0.940 (1.96)	0.631
Citizen liberal ideology	2.658 (1.68)	0.114	1.792 (1.35)	0.185
Total expenditure	−0.004 (0.00)	0.013	−0.006 (0.00)	0.001
Fiscal health ($1,000)	66.707 (50.51)	0.187	51.108 (50.99)	0.316
Federal transfer (%)	3.993 (1.94)	0.039	3.566 (2.11)	0.090
Debt burden (%)	−2.153 (0.80)	0.007	−2.345 (0.87)	0.007

Table 17 (cont.)

	Model 1		Model 2	
	Coefficient (Robust SE)	Two-tailed *p*-value	Coefficient (Robust SE)	Two-tailed *p*-value
Per capita personal income ($1,000)	−2.048 (3.11)	0.511	−2.549 (3.38)	0.450
Unemployment (%)	5.868 (3.88)	0.130	7.221 (3.81)	0.058
Population (1,000)	0.068 (0.03)	0.042	0.005 (0.04)	0.896
Constant	−369.907 (213.15)	0.083	89.981 (251.98)	0.721
Observations	550		550	
Wald χ^2	1,728.17		1,431.82	

Note: Two-tailed *p*-values. The dependent variable is the amount of money a state spends on lobbying in a year ($1,000s).

However, the effects of legislative professionalism were positive but statistically insignificant. This finding is reasonable as legislative professionalism was stable during the observation period, and the theoretical effects of legislative professionalism on state lobbying spending are probably not linearly additive. Therefore, compared to the models in Section 3, estimating the effect of legislative professionalism in a dynamic panel-data model with a non-log-transformed dependent variable is less statistically efficient. Following Shipan and Volden (2006), I also tested the interaction effects between legislative professionalism and local lobbying spending. The results (not reported here) were positive but not statistically significant. Moreover, there was no substantial evidence to confirm the potential effects of other political, financial, and demographic controls.

I provided additional analysis in Table 18 to verify one potential mechanism behind the snowball effect hypothesis. As mentioned before, state governments might compete with local governments for federal funding due to the unaligned political incentives of state and local policymakers. Goldstein and You (2017) also report that blue cities in red states are the most likely to participate in the federal government. Therefore, in Table 18, I replicated Model 2 by limiting the sample to pro-conservative states (i.e., government liberal ideology < 50) or states with citizens more liberal than the government (i.e., citizen liberal ideology – government liberal ideology > 0). Indeed, I found greater point estimates (0.080 and 0.093) in Models 3 and 4 than in Model 2 (0.069). This finding provides empirical support for the mechanism of unaligned political incentives of state and local policymakers.

4.3 Summary

Economics, political science, public administration, and public policy scholars have paid increasing attention to intergovernmental policy dependency in recent years (Graham, Shipan, and Volden 2013). Researchers have provided abundant evidence to illustrate the patterns of state-to-state and national-to-state policy dependency. However, there is considerably less research on local-to-state policy influence. Moreover, existing quantitative research on intergovernmental lobbying rarely examines the lobbying activities of state governments.

In this section, I present evidence of local-to-state diffusion in intergovernmental lobbying. Following Shipan and Vodlen (2006), I point out that two distinct effects can lead to bottom-up federalism in intergovernmental lobbying: the snowball effect and the pressure valve effect. Local lobbying spending may have a snowball effect on state lobbying spending by increasing the salience of lobbying as a policy tool and the negative externalities among local

Table 18 Arellano–Bond dynamic panel-data estimation of state lobbying spending (government liberal ideology < 50 or citizen liberal ideology – government liberal ideology > 0)

	Model 3		Model 4	
	Coefficient (Robust SE)	Two-tailed *p*-value	Coefficient (Robust SE)	Two-tailed *p*-value
Local lobbying spending ($1,000)	0.080 (0.02)	0.000	0.093 (0.03)	0.001
Lagged state lobbying spending ($1,000)	0.508 (0.06)	0.000	0.624 (0.12)	0.000
MDS 1	3.411 (94.91)	0.971	1.271 (87.65)	0.988
MDS 2	−15.147 (59.18)	0.798	−53.372 (72.22)	0.460
Gubernatorial election year	4.586 (10.42)	0.660	−21.656 (11.02)	0.049
Democrat governor	48.123 (54.99)	0.382	−3.213 (74.21)	0.965
Government liberal ideology	−0.778 (2.19)	0.722	3.271 (2.47)	0.186
Citizen liberal ideology	−0.565 (1.34)	0.672	2.140 (1.63)	0.188
Total expenditure	−0.005 (0.00)	0.092	−0.009 (0.00)	0.002
Fiscal health ($1,000)	95.930 (81.52)	0.239	33.447 (81.71)	0.682

Federal transfer (%)	4.792 (3.14)	0.127	3.106 (2.84)	0.275
Debt burden (%)	-2.065 (1.29)	0.110	-2.570 (1.13)	0.023
Per capita personal income ($1,000)	-1.802 (3.93)	0.647	0.110 (3.89)	0.977
Unemployment (%)	-1.237 (7.41)	0.867	7.376 (5.57)	0.186
Population (1,000)	-0.036 (0.04)	0.373	0.031 (0.06)	0.625
Constant	435.511 (325.27)	0.181	-135.096 (389.94)	0.729
Observations	289		342	
Wald χ^2	300.13		272.13	

Note: Two-tailed p-values. The dependent variable is the amount of money a state spends on lobbying in a year ($1,000s).

governments or escalating the competition for scarce federal funding between state and local governments. However, local lobbying spending may also produce a pressure valve effect on state lobbying spending by successfully reducing the policy demands and policy pressures from local voters and interest groups. The results of the empirical analysis of fifty states from 1999 to 2011 show that when local government lobbying spending increases, state lobbying spending also increases. In other words, it is the snowball effect rather than the pressure valve effect that dominates bottom-up federalism in intergovernmental lobbying.

This work contributes to our understanding of lobbying, policy diffusion, and intergovernmental relations. Previous quantitative intergovernmental lobbying research often focuses on how local governments allocate resources for lobbying the federal government, paying little or no attention to the potential effects of local lobbying investment on state lobbying investment (Goldstein and You 2017; Loftis and Kettler 2015; Payson 2020a, 2020b). Additionally, most diffusion research focuses on horizontal policy interdependency using regulatory policy cases (Graham, Shipan, and Volden 2013). Studies of the vertical interaction between state and local policies remain limited, and we still know little about when and how local actions influence state actions (Shipan and Volden 2006). To my knowledge, this study represents the first systematic analysis of vertical policy interdependency in the process of intergovernmental lobbying.

This analysis points to several other directions for future research. This study was limited by a lack of data availability and, therefore, did not differentiate between the effects of the multiple mechanisms behind the snowball effect. In other words, although this section provides evidence to suggest that bottom-up federalism exists in intergovernmental lobbying, we still do not know whether state governments respond to local governments because of proactive learning or as a passive response to policy pressures. Future researchers may use survey methods to obtain more first-hand information on the intergovernmental lobbying process to disentangle these mechanisms.

Moreover, bottom-up federalism may be more applicable to some lobbying issues than others. Future research with more fine-grained information may test bottom-up federalism of lobbying decisions in various specific policy areas to isolate different bottom-up diffusion mechanisms. Further, this section examines only one aspect of the state lobbying process: lobbying spending. Although the evaluation of state lobbying impact is beyond the scope of this study, this issue is the next logical step to be taken in the study of state lobbying activities.

Finally, future research could build on this work and explore the potential top-down or peer effects underlying intergovernmental lobbying activities.

Multiple policy diffusion studies have pointed out that superior governments can use coercive powers, administrative mandates, financial incentives, or policy discussions to influence the decisions of lower-level governments (McCann, Shipan, and Volden 2015; Tolbert and Zucker 1983; Zhang and Zhu 2020). Moreover, one local government's policy decision is often influenced by its peers through multiple mechanisms, such as learning, competition, and imitation (Shipan and Volden 2008). In the case of lobbying, for instance, a city may increase lobbying activities in response to state or other cities' efforts. Future research might further apply these theoretical insights to examining the potential interdependence patterns of the lobbying decisions among subnational governments.

5 Conclusion

5.1 Highlights of the Main Findings

The vast research literature on lobbying seeks to explain the origins, strategies, content, and consequences of lobbying activities among private interest groups (De Figueiredo and Richter 2014). However, much less attention is paid to the process of intergovernmental lobbying. Given that hundreds of subnational governments spend tens of millions of dollars on formally lobbying the federal government each year and these lobbying investments probably have significant impacts on national politics, a systematic analysis of the intergovernmental formal lobbying process is important and relevant.

This Element comprises three sections identifying and quantitatively testing the institutional origins of intergovernmental lobbying activities to improve our understanding of formal intergovernmental lobbying. Section 2 represents the first institutional analysis of the motivations and resources of government executives during intergovernmental lobbying. Section 2 reveals that cities with professional executives have a longer time horizon and more policy and administration expertise than those with political executives. Therefore, they have more incentive to allocate resources for lobbying the federal government. An analysis of the 1,259 largest cities in the United States between 1999 and 2012 suggests that, after controlling for political, financial, and demographic characteristics, executive institutions still significantly predict city lobbying participation and spending.

Section 3 represents one of the first quantitative analyses of state government lobbying activities. I argue that professional state legislatures are more likely to represent the preferences of the median voters and have more time, staff, and discretionary resources necessary for facilitating the formal lobbying process. Using a panel dataset covering fifty states from 1999 to 2011, I found that legislative professionalism was positively associated with state lobbying participation and spending.

Section 4 represents the first systematic analysis of bottom-up federalism in the case of intergovernmental lobbying. Borrowing the concept of bottom-up federalism from the policy diffusion literature, I argue that more local lobbying spending can lead to more or less state lobbying spending through a snowball or a pressure valve effect. A dynamic panel-data model of fifty states from 1999 to 2011 shows that when local governments increase their investments in lobbying the federal government by $1,000, state governments increase their investments in lobbying the federal government by $69 in the same year. This finding suggests that the snowball effect dominates the process of bottom-up federalism in intergovernmental lobbying.

5.2 Theoretical and Practical Implications

Several theoretical and practical implications can be drawn from this Element. First, different from previous demand-based explanations, such as ideological divergence or public demands (Goldstein and You 2017; Loftis and Kettler 2015), this study provides the first attempt to establish a theoretical logic that associates the institutional motivations or constraints of policymakers with the activities of intergovernmental lobbying. Exploring the factors underlying intergovernmental lobbying could help researchers better understand the role of intergovernmental lobbying in democratic representation and federalist governance. Moreover, this study follows the approach of recent quantitative intergovernmental lobbying research. It paves the way for systematically studying the impact of subnational institutions on intergovernmental lobbying decisions, given the inherent limits of most of the existing anecdotal or case studies (Jensen 2018). Nevertheless, causal inference in institutional analysis is difficult due to the lack of detailed information on causal mechanisms or valid counterfactual cases (Acemoglu, Gallego, and Robinson 2014; Capoccia and Kelemen 2007; Falleti and Lynch 2009; Grose and Wood 2020; Lieberman 2001). Notably, the statistical relationships shown in this study are correlations rather than empirical causations due to the data limitations. Therefore, more rigorous causal institutional analysis should be encouraged in future research.

Second, this study could help understand intergovernmental relations and federalism better. There is a long-standing debate on the structure of intergovernmental relations in the United States. Three models of intergovernmental relations have been proposed (Wright 1978): the coordinate-authority model in which subnational governments are independent of the national government and operate autonomously; the inclusive-authority model in which the subnational government are mere dependents of the national government; and the overlapping-authority model in which different tiers of government are interdependent, and intergovernmental interactions follow a bargaining authority pattern instead of an autonomic or hierarchic pattern. As subnational governments tend to lobby the federal government to obtain a larger slice of the federal budget or contracts, this study supports the overlapping-authority model by revealing how subnational governments interact or cooperate with the federal government through lobbying. Moreover, as a form of intergovernmental interaction, formal lobbying can influence the relations between different governments (Leckrone 2019). Formal intergovernmental lobbying may determine who has more voice in national politics and who shapes democratic representation and the distribution of federal resources in the country. The potential conflicts between paid and elected representation could significantly shape government responsiveness, performance, and legitimacy. This study's exploration of local governments' participation and investment in formal intergovernmental lobbying can provide a foundation for further identifying the determinants of intergovernmental relations and social equity.

Third, this study also contributes to the literature on urban politics, state politics, and public finance and management. It shows that urban and state institutional structures could significantly shape governmental lobbying decisions and may have broader implications regarding local and state financial allocation processes. Unlike typical local public projects (e.g., parks, roads, or schools), lobbying activities are largely invisible, and lobbying benefits are highly uncertain and tend to be produced in the long term. Studying local leaders' decisions on formal intergovernmental lobbying can shed new light on how and why local governments allocate resources for this type of expenditure. Furthermore, public management scholars tend to view intergovernmental networking as an important determinant of public organization performance (O'Toole and Meier 1999; Meier and O'Toole 2001). However, little research has discussed the origins of managerial networking in public administration (Rabovsky and Rutherford 2016). As federal lobbying spending is an objective measure of government managerial networking, this study also sheds some new light on the explanations for managerial networking in public administration research.

Fourth, the patterns of intergovernmental lobbying identified in this study could potentially be generalized to other contexts. Generally, in countries with a multilevel power structure, the distribution of various resources along government hierarchies tends to be imbalanced, and the upper-level governments often have limited information on local demands (Zhu and Zhang 2019). Under these circumstances, the lower-level governments are incentivized to lobby the upper-level governments for additional resources. Studying the dynamics and mechanisms of these activities could improve the academic knowledge of government behaviors and help practitioners promote or revise specific institutional designs to address social injustice issues produced by the unequal allocation of national resources.

5.3 Concluding Thoughts on a Future Research Agenda

There are multiple directions for future research. First, although the quantitative results have revealed multiple theoretically plausible mechanisms underlying the main hypotheses, some of them cannot be directly empirically verified given the current data or resource limits. For example, due to the lack of an established individual-level executive database of thousands of American cities in the past decades, it is difficult to verify whether all political executives have a shorter time horizon or less policy administration training or experience than professional executives. There is also insufficient information to systematically analyze the effects of local executive expertise or state legislative professionalism on transaction costs during the intergovernmental lobbying process. Moreover, it is difficult to determine empirically whether state government lobbying spending responds to local lobbying spending due to the increasing salience of lobbying as a policy tool, the negative externality of local lobbying activities, or the growing competition between state and local governments for the scarce federal funding. Researchers with better data or more resources may build on this study to further verify or develop these theoretical mechanisms.

Second, it should be reiterated that the two dependent variables this study attempts to explain are lobbying participation and spending, not specific proposals, actions, or policies during the lobbying process. Due to the difficulty of collecting more nuanced lobbying data, this work and other recent quantitative studies (Goldstein and You 2017; Loftis and Kettler 2015; Payson 2020a, 2020b) have mainly focused on examining the institutional or socioeconomic origins of intergovernmental lobbying participation or expenditure. Therefore, I encourage future research with in-depth data to further explore the possible strategies, contents, and consequences of intergovernmental lobbying to deepen our understanding of this topic. For instance, are there differences in the focus of lobbying efforts among subnational governments? What explains those differences? Why do some cities respond more quickly to crises through lobbying federal officials than others? More in-depth case studies and detailed content analyses are needed to strengthen the assessment of the determinants of specific lobbying decisions and behaviors. This study's exploration of the institutional origins of subnational governments' participation and investment in intergovernmental lobbying can provide a foundation for future research focusing on those research questions.

Third, we currently know little about how and why governmental interest groups behave differently from private interest groups during the lobbying process. Where public ownership is considered, it is treated as a rival explanation to control for rather than as the analytical focus (De Figueiredo and Silverman 2006). Consequently, the role of public ownership in the lobbying literature has been underdeveloped (Konisky and Teodoro 2016). Nevertheless, institutional ownership may determine each actor's motivation for participation, their decision to lobby, and constraints in the lobbying process. Therefore, the following questions merit examination in future research: Is the process of governmental lobbying different from private interest groups lobbying? How and why?

Fourth, the characteristics of a policy issue can have a significant impact on the actors involved in the policy process (Hayes 1981; Lowi 1972). For example, lobbyists may play different roles in the distributive, constituent, regulative, or redistributive policy sectors. Further, previous research suggests that the lobbying agenda tends to be significantly different from the congressional agenda (Baumgartner et al. 2009). However, the salience of a policy issue on the congressional agenda should at least partially determine the importance of an issue on the lobbying agenda. Therefore, future research with fine-grained information on issue-specific lobbying spending can further examine whether issue characteristics matter and whether the effects of institutions vary under different circumstances.

Finally, understanding how lobbying works in practice can help complement the quantitative analysis by adding traction to the causality underlying the statistical data analysis. With sufficient resources or funding, more field observations and qualitative interviews with the leaders of subnational governments and professional lobbyists should be encouraged (Baumgartner et al. 2009; Jensen 2018; Nownes 2006). As the US-style professional lobbying market is not necessarily popular or legal in other contexts, comparative studies of formal or informal lobbying activities with cases from other countries can help produce otherwise ignored insights.

References

Abramoff, Jack. 2011. *Capitol Punishment: The Hard Truth about Washington Corruption from America's Most Notorious Lobbyist*. Washington, DC: WND.

Acemoglu, Daron, Francisco A. Gallego, and James A. Robinson. 2014. Institutions, Human Capital, and Development. *Annual Review of Economics* 6(1): 875–912.

Akaike, Hirotugu. 1974. A New Look at the Statistical Model Identification. *IEEE Transactions on Automatic Control* 19: 716–723.

Akiashvili, Lela, Humna Butt, Kirbie Ferrell et al. 2018. *Lobbying After Federal Service: The Revolving Door, Shadow Lobbying, and Cooling Off Periods for Former Government Officials*. 2017–2018 CRS Consulting Capstone Team (Advisor: Deborah L. Kerr), The Bush School of Government and Public Service, Texas A&M University. http://bush.tamu.edu/psaa/cap stones/2018/CRS%20Exec%20Branch%20Lobbying%20Capstone%20Final %20Report%202017-2018.pdf

Alesina, Alberto and Guido Tabellini. 2007. Bureaucrats or Politicians? Part I: A Single Policy Task. *American Economic Review* 97(1): 169–179.

Alesina, Alberto and Guido Tabellini. 2008. Bureaucrats or Politicians? Part II: Multiple Policy Tasks. *Journal of Public Economics* 92 (3–4): 426–447.

Ammons, David N. and Matthew J. Bosse. 2005. Tenure of City Managers: Examining the Dual Meanings of "Average Tenure." *State and Local Government Review* 37(1): 61–71.

Arellano, Manuel and Stephen Bond. 1991. Some Tests of Specification for Panel Data: Monte Carlo Evidence and An Application to Employment Equations. *The Review of Economic Studies* 58(2): 277–297.

Barber, Michael and Adam M. Dynes. 2019. City-State Ideological Incongruence and Municipal Preemption. *American Journal of Political Science*. https://onlinelibrary.wiley.com/doi/full/10.1111/ajps.12655

Bardhan, Pranab. 2002. Decentralization of Governance and Development. *Journal of Economic Perspectives* 16(4): 185–205.

Baumgartner, Frank R., Jeffrey M. Berry, Marie Hojnacki, Beth L. Leech, and David C. Kimball. 2009. *Lobbying and Policy Change: Who Wins, Who Loses, and Why*. Chicago, IL: University of Chicago Press.

Berry, Frances Stokes and William D. Berry. 1990. State Lottery Adoptions as Policy Innovations: An Event History Analysis. *American Political Science Review* 84(2): 395–415.

Berry, William D., Michael B. Berkman, and Stuart Schneiderman. 2000. Legislative Professionalism and Incumbent Reelection: The Development of Institutional Boundaries. *American Political Science Review* 94(4): 859–874.

Berry, William D., Richard C. Fording, Evan J. Ringquist, Russell L. Hanson, and Carl E. Klarner. 2010. Measuring Citizen and Government Ideology in the US States: A Re-Appraisal. *State Politics & Policy Quarterly* 10(2): 117–135.

Bertelli, Anthony M. and Peter John. 2013. Public Policy Investment: Risk and Return in British Politics. *British Journal of Political Science* 43(4): 741–773.

Bertrand, Marianne, Matilde Bombardini, and Francesco Trebbi. 2014. Is It Whom You Know or What You Know? An Empirical Assessment of the Lobbying Process. *American Economic Review* 104(12): 3885–3920.

Besley, Timothy and Stephen Coate. 2003. Centralized versus Decentralized Provision of Local Public Goods: A Political Economy Approach. *Journal of Public Economics* 87(12): 2611–2637.

Borisov, Alexander, Eitan Goldman, and Nandini Gupta. 2016. The Corporate Value of (Corrupt) Lobbying. *The Review of Financial Studies* 29(4): 1039–1071.

Bowen, Daniel C. and Zachary Greene. 2014. Should We Measure Professionalism with An Index? A Note on Theory and Practice in State Legislative Professionalism Research. *State Politics & Policy Quarterly* 14 (3): 277–296.

Box-Steffensmeier, Janet M., Dino P. Christenson, and Alison W. Craig. 2019. Cue-Taking in Congress: Interest Group Signals from Dear Colleague Letters. *American Journal of Political Science* 63(1): 163–180.

Brooks, Glenn E. 1961. *When Governors Convene: The Governors' Conference and National Politics*. Baltimore, MA: Johns Hopkins Press.

Bueno, Natalia. 2021. The Timing of Public Policies: Political Budget Cycles and Credit Claiming. *American Journal of Political Science*. https://onlinelibrary .wiley.com/doi/full/10.1111/ajps.12688

Cammisa, Anne Marie. 1995. *Governments as Interest Groups: Intergovernmental Lobbying and the Federal System*. Westport, CT: Praeger.

Capoccia, Giovanni and R. Daniel Kelemen. 2007. The Study of Critical Junctures: Theory, Narrative, and Counterfactuals in Historical Institutionalism. *World Politics* 59(3): 341–369.

Carr, Jered B. 2015. What Have We Learned about the Performance of Council-Manager Government? A Review and Synthesis of the Research. *Public Administration Review* 75(5): 673–689.

Carreri, Maria and Julia Payson. 2021. What Makes a Good Local Leader? Evidence from US Mayors and City Managers. *Journal of Political Institutions and Political Economy* 2(2): 199–225.

Carsey, Thomas M., Jonathan Winburn, and William D. Berry. 2017. Rethinking the Normal Vote, the Personal Vote, and the Impact of Legislative Professionalism in US State Legislative Elections. *State Politics & Policy Quarterly* 17(4): 465–488.

Clark, William Roberts, Matt Golder, and Sona N Golder. 2017. The British Academy Brian Barry Prize Essay: An Exit, Voice, and Loyalty Model of Politics. *British Journal of Political Science* 47(4): 719–748.

Clingermayer, James C. and Richard C. Feiock. 2001. *Institutional Constraints and Policy Choice: An Exploration of Local Governance*. Albany, NY: State University of New York Press.

Connolly, Jennifer M. 2016. The Impact of Local Politics on the Principal-Agent Relationship between Council and Manager in Municipal Government. *Journal of Public Administration Research and Theory* 27(2): 253–268.

De Benedictis-Kessner, Justin and Christopher Warshaw. 2016. Mayoral Partisanship and Municipal Fiscal Policy. *Journal of Politics* 78(4): 1124–1138.

De Figueiredo, John M. and Brian Kelleher Richter. 2014. Advancing the Empirical Research on Lobbying. *Annual Review of Political Science* 17: 163–185.

De Figueiredo, John M. and Brian S. Silverman. 2006. Academic Earmarks and the Returns to Lobbying. *The Journal of Law and Economics* 49(2): 597–625.

Dekel, Eddie, Matthew O. Jackson, and Asher Wolinsky. 2009. Vote Buying: Legislatures and Lobbying. *Quarterly Journal of Political Science* 4(2): 103–128.

Ellis, Christopher J. and Thomas Groll. 2020. Strategic Legislative Subsidies: Informational Lobbying and the Cost of Policy. *American Political Science Review* 114(1): 179–205.

Falleti, Tulia G. and Julia F. Lynch. 2009. Context and Causal Mechanisms in Political Analysis. *Comparative Political Studies* 42(9): 1143–1166.

Farkas, Suzanne. 1971. *Urban Lobbying: Mayors in the Federal Arena*. New York: New York University Press.

Feiock, Richard C., Moon-Gi Jeong, and Jaehoon Kim. 2003. Credible Commitment and Council Manager Government: Implications for Policy Instrument Choices. *Public Administration Review* 63(5): 616–625.

Fiorina, Morris P. and Roger G. Noll. 1978a. Voters, Bureaucrats and Legislators: A Rational Choice Perspective on the Growth of Bureaucracy. *Journal of Public Economics* 9(2): 239–254.

Fiorina, Morris P. and Roger G. Noll. 1978b. Voters, Legislators and Bureaucracy: Institutional Design in the Public Sector. *The American Economic Review* 68(2): 256–260.

Fortunato, David and Ian R. Turner. 2018. Legislative Capacity and Credit Risk. *American Journal of Political Science* 62(3): 623–636.

Gilardi, Fabrizio. 2010. Who Learns from What in Policy Diffusion Processes? *American Journal of Political Science* 54(3): 650–666.

Gill, Jeff and Christopher Witko. 2013. Bayesian Analytical Methods: A Methodological Prescription for Public Administration. *Journal of Public Administration Research and Theory* 23(2): 457–494.

Goldstein, Rebecca and Hye Young You. 2017. Cities as Lobbyists. *American Journal of Political Science* 61(4): 864–876.

Gordon, Rebecca H. and Thomas M. Susman. 2009. The Lobbying Manual: A Complete Guide to Federal Lobbying Law and Practice. New York: American Bar Association.

Graham, Erin R., Charles R. Shipan, and Craig Volden. 2013. The Diffusion of Policy Diffusion Research in Political Science. *British Journal of Political Science* 43(3): 673–701.

Gray, Virginia. 1973. Innovation in the States: A Diffusion Study. *The American Political Science Review* 67(4): 1174–1185.

Gray, Virginia. 1994. Competition, Emulation, and Policy Innovation. In Lawrence C. Dodd and Calvin C. Jillson (eds.) *New Perspectives on American Politics* (pp. 230–248). Washington, DC: CQ Press.

Gray, Virginia and David Lowery. 1996. *The Population Ecology of Interest Representation: Lobbying Communities in the American States.* Ann Arbor, MI: University of Michigan Press.

Grose, Christian R. and Abby K. Wood. 2020. Randomized Experiments by Government Institutions and American Political Development. *Public Choice* 185(3): 401–413.

Grose, Christian R., Pamela Lopez, Sara Sadhwani, and Antoine Yoshinaka. 2022. Social Lobbying. *Journal of Politics* 84(1): 1–16.

Haeder, Simon F. and Susan Webb Yackee. 2015. Influence and the Administrative Process: Lobbying the US President's Office of Management and Budget. *American Political Science Review* 109(03): 507–522.

Haider, Donald H. 1974. *When Governments Come to Washington: Governors, Mayors, and Intergovernmental Lobbying.* New York: The Free Press.

Hall, Richard L. and Alan V. Deardorff. 2006. Lobbying as Legislative Subsidy. *American Political Science Review* 100(01): 69–84.

Hayes, Michael T. 1981. *Lobbyists and Legislators: A Theory of Political Markets.* New Brunswick, NJ: Rutgers University Press.

Hayes, Kathy and Semoon Chang. 1990. The Relative Efficiency of City Manager and Mayor-Council Forms of Government. *Southern Economic Journal* 57(1): 167–177.

Hayes, Michael T. 1992. *Incrementalism and Public Policy.* New York: Longman.

Hays, R. Allen. 1991. Intergovernmental Lobbying: Toward an Understanding of Issue Priorities. *Western Political Quarterly* 44(4): 1081–1098.

Herian, Mitchel N. 2011. *Governing the States and the Nation: The Intergovernmental Policy Influence of the National Governors Association.* Amherst, NY: Cambria Press.

Hirschman, Albert O. 1970. *Exit, Voice, and Loyalty: Responses to Decline in Firms, Organizations, and States.* Cambridge, MA: Harvard University Press.

Ho, Daniel E., Kosuke Imai, Gary King, and Elizabeth A. Stuart. 2007. Matching as Nonparametric Preprocessing for Reducing Model Dependence in Parametric Causal Inference. *Political Analysis* 15(3): 199–236.

Jansa, Joshua M., Eric R. Hansen, and Virginia H. Gray. 2019. Copy and Paste Lawmaking: Legislative Professionalism and Policy Reinvention in the States. *American Politics Research* 47(4): 739–767.

Jensen, Jennifer M. 2016. *The Governors' Lobbyists: Federal-State Relations Offices and Governors Associations in Washington.* Ann Arbor, MI: University of Michigan Press.

Jensen, Jennifer M. 2018. Intergovernmental Lobbying in the United States: Assessing the Benefits of Accumulated Knowledge. *State and Local Government Review* 50(4): 270–281.

Jensen, Jennifer M. and Jenna Kelkres Emery. 2011. The First State Lobbyists: State Offices in Washington During World War II. *Journal of Policy History* 23(2): 117–149.

Kang, Karam. 2016. Policy Influence and Private Returns from Lobbying in the Energy Sector. *The Review of Economic Studies* 83(1): 269–305.

Karch, Andrew. 2007. *Democratic Laboratories: Policy Diffusion among the American States.* Ann Arbor, MI: University of Michigan Press.

Karch, Andrew. 2012. Vertical Diffusion and the Policy-Making Process: The Politics of Embryonic Stem Cell Research. *Political Research Quarterly* 65 (1): 48–61.

Karch, Andrew and Aaron Rosenthal. 2016. Vertical Diffusion and the Shifting Politics of Electronic Commerce. *State Politics & Policy Quarterly* 16(1): 22–43.

Kiewiet, D. Roderick and Mathew D. McCubbins. 2014. State and Local Government Finance: The New Fiscal Ice Age. *Annual Review of Political Science* 17: 105–122.

Kim, In Song. 2017. Political Cleavages Within Industry: Firm-Level Lobbying for Trade Liberalization. *American Political Science Review* 111(1): 1–20.

King, James D. 2000. Changes in Professionalism in US State Legislatures. *Legislative Studies Quarterly* 25(2): 327–343.

Kingdon, John W. 1984. *Agendas, Alternatives, and Public Policies.* Boston, MA: Little, Brown.

Kirk, Robert S., William J. Mallett, and David Randall Peterman. 2017. *Transportation Spending Under an Earmark Ban.* Congressional Research Service Report Prepared for Members and Committees of Congress: January 4. https://fas.org/sgp/crs/misc/R41554.pdf

Kirkland, Patricia A. 2021, Business Owners and Executives as Politicians: The Effect on Public Policy. *Journal of Politics* 83(4): 1652–1668.

Kollman, Ken. 1997. Inviting Friends to Lobby: Interest Groups, Ideological Bias, and Congressional Committees. *American Journal of Political Science* 41(2): 519–544.

Konisky, David M. and Manuel P. Teodoro. 2016. When Governments Regulate Governments. *American Journal of Political Science* 60(3): 559–574.

Krause, Rachel M., Christopher V. Hawkins, Angela Y.S. Park, and Richard C. Feiock. 2019. Drivers of Policy Instrument Selection for Environmental Management by Local Governments. *Public Administration Review* 79(4): 477–487.

Krebs, Timothy B. and John P. Pelissero. 2010. Urban Managers and Public Policy: Do Institutional Arrangements Influence Decisions to Initiate Policy? *Urban Affairs Review* 45(3): 391–411.

Lieberman, Evan S. 2001. Causal Inference in Historical Institutional Analysis: A Specification of Periodization Strategies. *Comparative Political Studies* 34 (9): 1011–1035.

LaPira, Timothy. 2015. Lobbying in the Shadows: How Private Interests Hide from Public Scrutiny and Why That Matters. In Cigler, Allan J., Burdett A. Loomis, and Anthony J. Nownes (eds.) *Interest Group Politics* (p. 225). Washington, DC: CQ Press.

LaPira, Timothy M. and Herschel F. Thomas III. 2014. Revolving Door Lobbyists and Interest Representation. *Interest Groups & Advocacy* 3(1): 4–29.

Lei, Zhenhuan and Junlong Aaron Zhou. 2022. Private Returns to Public Investment: Political Career Incentives and Infrastructure Investment in China. *Journal of Politics* 84(1): 1–15.

Loftis, Matt W. and Jaclyn J. Kettler. 2015. Lobbying from Inside the System: Why Local Governments Pay for Representation in the US Congress. *Political Research Quarterly* 68(1): 193–206.

Lowi, Theodore J. 1972. Four Systems of Policy, Politics, and Choice. *Public Administration Review* 32(4): 298–310.

Lubell, Mark, Richard C. Feiock, and Edgar E. Ramirez De La Cruz. 2009. Local Institutions and the Politics of Urban Growth. *American Journal of Political Science* 53(3): 649–665.

Lynn, Laurence E. Jr. 1987. *Managing Public Policy.* Boston, MA: Little Brown.

Maestas, Cherie. 2000. Professional Legislatures and Ambitious Politicians: Policy Responsiveness of State Institutions. *Legislative Studies Quarterly* 25 (4): 663–690.

Malhotra, Neil. 2006. Government Growth and Professionalism in US State Legislatures. *Legislative Studies Quarterly* 31(4): 563–584.

Martin, David L. 1990. *Running City Hall: Municipal Administration in America.* Tuscaloosa, AL: University of Alabama Press.

McCabe, Barbara Coyle, Richard C. Feiock, James C. Clingermayer, and Christopher Stream. 2008. Turnover among City Managers: The Role of Political and Economic Change. *Public Administration Review* 68(2): 380–386.

McCann, Pamela J. Clouser, Charles R. Shipan, and Craig Volden. 2015. Top-Down Federalism: State Policy Responses to National Government Discussions. *Publius* 45(4): 495–525.

McCrain, Joshua. 2018. Revolving Door Lobbyists and the Value of Congressional Staff Connections. *Journal of Politics* 80(4): 1369–1383.

McFadden, Daniel. 1974. Conditional Logit Analysis of Qualitative Choice Behavior. In Paul Zarembka (ed.) *Frontiers in Econometrics* (pp. 105–142). New York: Academic Press.

McNitt, Andrew Douglas. 2010. Tenure in Office of Big City Mayors. *State and Local Government Review* 42(1): 36–47.

Meier, Kenneth J. and Laurence J. O'Toole. 2001. Managerial Strategies and Behavior in Networks: A Model with Evidence from US Public Education. *Journal of Public Administration Research and Theory* 11(3): 271–294.

Meltzer, Allan H. and Scott F. Richard. 1981. A Rational Theory of the Size of Government. *Journal of Political Economy* 89(5): 914–927.

Meltzer, Allan H. and Scott F. Richard. 1983. Tests of a Rational Theory of the Size of Government. *Public Choice* 41(3): 403–418.

Mooney, Christopher Z. 1995. Citizens, Structures, and Sister States: Influences on State Legislative Professionalism. *Legislative Studies Quarterly* 20(1): 47–67.

Mullin, Megan, Gillian Peele, and Bruce E. Cain. 2004. City Caesars? Institutional Structure and Mayoral Success in Three California Cities. *Urban Affairs Review* 40(1): 19–43.

Nicholson-Crotty, Sean. 2015. *Governors, Grants, and Elections: Fiscal Federalism in the American States*. Baltimore, MA: John Hopkins University Press.

Nixon, H.C. 1944. The Southern Governors' Conference as a Pressure Group. *Journal of Politics* 6(3): 338–345.

Nownes, Anthony J. 1999. Solicited Advice and Lobbyist Power: Evidence from Three American States. *Legislative Studies Quarterly* 24(1): 113–123.

Nownes, Anthony J. 2006. Total Lobbying: What Lobbyists Want (and How They Try to Get It). New York: Cambridge University Press.

Oates, Wallace E. 1999. An Essay on Fiscal Federalism. *Journal of Economic Literature* 37(3): 1120–1149.

Olson, Mancur. 1965. *The Logic of Collective Action*. Cambridge, MA: Harvard University Press.

Olson, Mancur. 1993. Dictatorship, Democracy, and Development. *American Political Science Review* 87(3): 567–576.

O'Toole, Laurence J. and Kenneth J. Meier. 1999. Modeling the Impact of Public Management: Implications of Structural Context. *Journal of Public Administration Research and Theory* 9(4): 505–526.

Owings, Stephanie and Rainald Borck. 2000. Legislative Professionalism and Government Spending: Do Citizen Legislators Really Spend Less? *Public Finance Review* 28(3): 210–225.

Palazzolo, Daniel J. and Fiona R. McCarthy. 2005. State and Local Government Organizations and the Formation of the Help America Vote Act. *Publius* 35 (4): 515–535.

Payson, Julia A. 2020a. Cities in the Statehouse: How Local Governments Use Lobbyists to Secure State Funding. *Journal of Politics* 82(2): 403–417.

Payson, Julia A. 2020b. The Partisan Logic of City Mobilization: Evidence from State Lobbying Disclosures. *American Political Science Review* 114(3): 677–690.

Pelissero, John P. and Robert E. England. 1987. State and Local Governments' Washington "Reps": Lobbying Strategies and President Reagan's New Federalism. *State and Local Government Review* 19(2): 68–72.

Pierson, Kawika, Michael L. Hand, and Fred Thompson. 2015. The Government Finance Database: A Common Resource for Quantitative Research in Public Financial Analysis. *PLoS ONE* 10(6): e0130119.

Rabovsky, Thomas and Amanda Rutherford. 2016. The Politics of Higher Education: University President Ideology and External Networking. *Public Administration Review* 76(5): 764–777.

Rainey, Carlisle. 2016. Dealing With Separation in Logistic Regression Models. *Political Analysis* 24(3): 339–355.

Rocco, Philip, Daniel Béland, and Alex Waddan. 2020. Stuck in Neutral? Federalism, Policy Instruments, and Counter-Cyclical Responses to COVID-19 in the United States. *Policy and Society* 39(3): 458–477.

Schattschneider, Elmer Eric and David Adamany. 1975. *The Semi-Sovereign People: A Realist's View of Democracy in America*. Hinsdale, IL: Dryden Press.

Schlozman, Kay Lehman. 1984. What Accent the Heavenly Chorus? Political Equality and the American Pressure System. *Journal of Politics* 46(4): 1006–1032.

Schnakenberg, Keith E. and Ian R. Turner. 2019. Signaling With Reform: How the Threat of Corruption Prevents Informed Policy-Making. *American Political Science Review* 113(3): 762–777.

Schwarz, Gideon. 1978. Estimating the Dimension of a Model. *The Annals of Statistics* 6(2): 461–464.

Shepherd, Michael E. and Hye Young You. 2020. Exit Strategy: Career Concerns and Revolving Doors in Congress. *American Political Science Review* 114(1): 270–284.

Shipan, Charles R. and Craig Volden. 2006. Bottom-Up Federalism: The Diffusion of Antismoking Policies from US Cities to States. *American Journal of Political Science* 50(4): 825–843.

Shipan, Charles R. and Craig Volden. 2008. The Mechanisms of Policy Diffusion. *American Journal of Political Science* 52(4): 840–857.

Shipan, Charles R. and Craig Volden. 2012. Policy Diffusion: Seven Lessons for Scholars and Practitioners. *Public Administration Review* 72(6): 788–796.

Shipan, Charles R. and Craig Volden. 2014. When the Smoke Clears: Expertise, Learning and Policy Diffusion. *Journal of Public Policy* 34(3): 357–387.

Shor, Boris and Nolan McCarty. 2011. The Ideological Mapping of American Legislatures. *American Political Science Review* 105(3): 530–551.

Squire, Peverill. 2017. A Squire Index Update. *State Politics & Policy Quarterly* 17(4): 361–371.

Squire, Peverill and Hamm, Keith E. 2005. *101 Chambers: Congress, State Legislatures, and the Future of Legislative Studies*. Columbus, OH: Ohio State University Press.

Stigler, George J. 1971. The Theory of Economic Regulation. *The Bell Journal of Economics and Management Science* 2(1): 3–21.

Straus, Jacob R. 2015. *The Lobbying Disclosure Act at 20: Analysis and Issues for Congress*. Congressional Research Service Report Prepared for Members and Committees of Congress: December 1. https://fas.org/sgp/crs/misc/R44292.pdf

Straus, Jacob R. 2017. *Lobbying Registration and Disclosure: The Role of the Clerk of the House and the Secretary of the Senate.* Congressional Research Service Report Prepared for Members and Committees of Congress: December 1. www.senate.gov/CRSpubs/63879f94-6966-4341-9342-03ab6d8bff33.pdf

Svara, James H. 1999. The Shifting Boundary between Elected Officials and City Managers in Large Council-Manager Cities. *Public Administration Review* 59(1): 44–53.

Teodoro, Manuel P. 2011. *Bureaucratic Ambition: Careers, Motives, and the Innovative Administrator.* Baltimore, MA: John Hopkins University Press.

Ting, Michael M. 2021. The Political Economy of Governance Quality. *American Political Science Review* 115(2): 667–685.

Tolbert, Pamela S. and Lynne G. Zucker. 1983. Institutional Sources of Change in the Formal Structure of Organizations: The Diffusion of Civil Service Reform, 1880–1935. *Administrative Science Quarterly* 28(1): 22–39.

Treisman, Daniel. 2007. *The Architecture of Government: Rethinking Political Decentralization.* Cambridge: Cambridge University Press.

Trounstine, Jessica. 2010. Representation and Accountability in Cities. *Annual Review of Political Science* 13: 407–423.

Trounstine, Jessica and Melody E. Valdini. 2008. The Context Matters: The Effects of Single-Member versus At-Large Districts on City Council Diversity. *American Journal of Political Science* 52(3): 554–569.

Vidal, Jordi Blanes i, Mirko Draca, and Christian Fons-Rosen. 2012. Revolving Door Lobbyists. *American Economic Review* 102(7): 3731–3348.

Volden, Craig. 2006. States as Policy Laboratories: Emulating Success in the Children's Health Insurance Program. *American Journal of Political Science* 50(2): 294–312.

Walker, Jack L. 1969. The Diffusion of Innovations among the American States. *The American Political Science Review* 63(3): 880–899.

Walker, Jack L. 1983. The Origins and Maintenance of Interest Groups in America. *American Political Science Review* 77: 390–406.

Walker, Jack L. 1991. *Mobilizing Interest Groups in America: Patrons, Professions, and Social Movements.* Ann Arbor, MI: University of Michigan Press.

Weingast, Barry R. 1996. Political Institutions: Rational Choice Perspectives. In Robert E. Goodin and Hans-Dieter Klingemann (eds.) *A New Handbook of Political Science* (pp. 167–190). New York: Oxford University Press.

Weingast, Barry R., Kenneth A. Shepsle, and Christopher Johnsen. 1981. The Political Economy of Benefits and Costs: A Neoclassical Approach to Distributive Politics. *The Journal of Political Economy* 89(4): 642–664.

Wesley Leckrone, J. 2019. Trying Not to Lose Ground: State and Local Government Advocacy During Passage of the 2017 Tax Cuts and Jobs Act. *Publius: The Journal of Federalism* 49(3): 407–436.

Wilensky, Harold L. 2015. *Organizational Intelligence: Knowledge and Policy in Government and Industry.* New Orleans, LA: Quid Pro Books.

Wright, Deil Spencer. 1978. *Understanding Intergovernmental Relations.* Belmont, CA: Duxbury Press.

Yackee, Susan Webb. 2006. Sweet-Talking the Fourth Branch: The Influence of Interest Group Comments on Federal Agency Rulemaking. *Journal of Public Administration Research and Theory* 16(1): 103–124.

Yackee, Susan Webb. 2020. Hidden Politics? Assessing Lobbying Success during US Agency Guidance Development. *Journal of Public Administration Research and Theory* 30(4): 548–562.

Yackee, Jason Webb and Susan Webb Yackee. 2006. A Bias Towards Business? Assessing Interest Group Influence on the US Bureaucracy. *Journal of Politics* 68(1): 128–139.

You, Hye Young. 2017. Ex Post Lobbying. *Journal of Politics* 79(4): 1162–1176.

Zhang, Yahong. 2007. *Local Official's Incentives and Policy-Making: Through the Lens of the Politics-Administration Relationship.* PhD Dissertation, Florida State University.

Zhang, Yahong and Richard C. Feiock. 2009. City Managers' Policy Leadership in Council-Manager Cities. *Journal of Public Administration Research and Theory* 20(2): 461–476.

Zhang, Youlang and Xufeng Zhu. 2020. The Moderating Role of Top-down Supports in Horizontal Innovation Diffusion. *Public Administration Review* 80(2): 209–221.

Zhu, Xufeng and Youlang Zhang. 2019. Diffusion of Marketization Innovation with Administrative Centralization in A Multilevel System: Evidence from China. *Journal of Public Administration Research and Theory* 29(1): 133–150.

Acknowledgements

This research was supported by the National Natural Science Foundation of China [Grant Number: 72004220], the Major Project of the National Social Science Foundation of China [Grant Number: 20ZDA042], and the fund for building world-class universities (disciplines) of Renmin University of China [Grant Number: KYGJD2022008]. The author would like to thank Dr. Manuel P. Teodoro for his guidance and support throughout this research. The author declares no conflict of interest.

About the Author

Youlang Zhang, Associate Professor, School of Public Administration and Policy | Capital Development and Governance Institute | Health science, hospital reform and medical big data liberal arts and sciences cross platform (team), Renmin University of China, Beijing, China. His research interests encompass policy process, citizen participation, and bureaucratic politics. His recent publications have appeared in *Journal of Public Administration Research and Theory, Public Administration Review, Governance, Public Administration, Policy Studies Journal*, among others.

Cambridge Elements ☰

Public and Nonprofit Administration

Andrew Whitford
University of Georgia

Andrew Whitford is Alexander M. Crenshaw Professor of Public Policy in the School of Public and International Affairs at the University of Georgia. His research centers on strategy and innovation in public policy and organization studies.

Robert Christensen
Brigham Young University

Robert Christensen is professor and George Romney Research Fellow in the Marriott School at Brigham Young University. His research focuses on prosocial and antisocial behaviors and attitudes in public and nonprofit organizations.

About the Series

The foundation of this series are cutting-edge contributions on emerging topics and definitive reviews of keystone topics in public and nonprofit administration, especially those that lack longer treatment in textbook or other formats. Among keystone topics of interest for scholars and practitioners of public and nonprofit administration, it covers public management, public budgeting and finance, nonprofit studies, and the interstitial space between the public and nonprofit sectors, along with theoretical and methodological contributions, including quantitative, qualitative and mixed-methods pieces.

The Public Management Research Association

The Public Management Research Association improves public governance by advancing research on public organizations, strengthening links among interdisciplinary scholars, and furthering professional and academic opportunities in public management.

Cambridge Elements ≡

Public and Nonprofit Administration

Printed in the United States
by Baker & Taylor Publisher Services